HUMANITIES

TRANSLATION :

FROM ENGLISH INTO ARABIC

ترجمة العلــوم الإنســانية:

من اللغة الإنجليزية إلى اللغة العربية

Dr. Muhammad Ali Alkhuli

Publisher : DAR ALFALAH P. o. Box 818 Swaileh 11910 Jordan Tel & fax 009626-5411547	الناشر: دار الفلاح للنشر والتوزيع ص. ب 818 11910 الأردن صويلح هاتف وفاكس 009626-5411547

E-mail: books @daralfalah.com
Website: www.daralfalah.com

2008 Edition

Publisher : DAR ALFALAH P.O. BOX 818 Swaileh 11910 Jordan Tel & Fax 009626-5411547	الناشر : دار الفلاح للنشر والتوزيع ص. ب 818 صويلح 11910 الأردن هاتف و فاكس 009626-5411547
E-mail: books@daralfalah.com Website: WWW.daralfalah.com	

رقم الإيداع لدى دائرة المكتبة الوطنية

2001/7/1373

418, 022

الخولي ، محمد علي

ترجمة العلوم الإنسانية : من اللغة العربية / محمد علي

الخولي . عَمُان : دار الفلاح ، 2001

(202) ص

ر. إ : 1373/ 7 /2001

المواصفات : الترجمة / العلوم الإنسانية / اللغة الإنجليزية .

● تم إعداد بيانات الفهرسة والتصنيف الأولية من قبل دائرة المكتبة الوطنية ، الأردن

رقم الإجازة المتسلسل لدى دائرة المطبوعات والنشر 1365 / 7 / 2001

ISBN 9957- 401- 39 - 4 (ردمك)

CONTENTS

بسم الله الرحمن الرحيم

PREFACE

مقدمـة

هذا الكتاب تدريب على ترجمة نصوص في العلوم الإنسانية والعلــوم الإجتماعية . ولذلك ، جاءت القطع فيه متنوعة من حيث موضوعاتها : التاريخ ، تاريخ الأدب ، اللغويات ، علم النفس ، الجغرافيا ،التربية ، علــم السياسة ، الفلسفة ، وعلم الإجتماع . وقد توزعت القطع على الموضوعــات التسعة بالتساوي تقريبا ، أي بمعدل خمس قطع لكل موضوع .

ويشمل الكتاب في بدايتة جزءاً تمهيدياً يتناول المبــادئ العامة في الترجمة . ويحسن بالأستاذ أن يوضح هذه المبادئ لطلابه قبل البدء بالترجمة . وبالطبع ، هناك مبادئ أخرى عديدة يمكن للأستاذ أن يوضــحها لطلابه كلما رأى ذلك مناسباً .

ولقد جعلتُ عدد الوحدات خمســاً وأربعيـــن وحدة لتساوي عـــدد المحاضرات في الفصل الدراسي الواحد ، على أساس ثــلاث محاضـــرات أسبوعياً على مدى خمســة عشـــر أسبوعاً في الفصل الدراسـي الواحد . هذا إذا

5

افترضنا تدريس 45 محاضرة . وإذا كان عدد المحاضرات أقل ، فإن هذا يمكّن الأستاذ من اختيار ما يشاء من القطع واستثناء ما يشاء .

ومن أفضل الطرق لتدريس الترجمة - في رأيـي - هـي أن يقـوم الطلاب بالترجمة المكتوبة خارج الصف ، ثم يقوم الطلاب بتدقيق الترجمـة بإشراف الأستاذ في أثناء المحاضرة ، ثم يقومون بكتابة الترجمـة النهائيـة خارج الصف . بعبارة أخرى ، هناك ثلاث مراحل : (1) كتابـة الطلاب للترجمة الأولى في البيت ، (2) تدقيق الترجمة بإشراف الأستاذ في الصف ، (3) كتابة الطلاب للترجمة النهائية في البيت . لا شك أن هناك طرقاً أخـرى لتدريس الترجمة ، ولكنني أعتقد أن هذه الطريقة من أفضل الطرق . وعلـى أي حال ، يحسن بالأستاذ أن يجرّب عدة طرق ويختار منها ما يروق له .

كل وحـدة في الكتاب تحتوي على نـص مـن صفحتيـن ، وهـي كميـة كافيـة في الغالب لملء ساعة من الزمن هي وقت المحاضرة . وفي الحقيقة ، قد لا يتمكن الأستاذ من ترجمة الصفحتين تحت ضغط الوقت . إن الأمر يتوقف على صعوبة النص وعلى مستوى الطلاب وعلى مـدى تحضـيرهم وعلـى طريقة تدريس الترجمة . لا شيء يلزم الأستاذ بترجمة الصفحتيـن ، إذ قـد يكتفي ببعض الفقرات أو إحدى الصفحتين . ولكن هناك مجـال مفتوح للطالب دائمـاً أن يترجم أكثر ما يستطيع من النص لأن لديه مجـالاً أوسـع من الوقـت خـارج الصف مما هو الحال في الصـف تحـت ضغط الوقت المحـدود للمحاضرة .

بالإضافة إلى النـص ، تحتوي كـل وحـدة علـى كلمات مساعدة Helpf Vocabulary . وتظهـر تحـت هذا العنـوان أهـم العبارات الواردة

6

في النص ، وتظهر أمام كل عبارة ترجمتها باللغة الـهدف حسـبما يتطلـب السياق ، وهي عبارات اصطلاحية في الغالب . هذه الصفحة مـن الكلمـات المساعدة لا تحتوي على كل المفردات والعبارات التـي يحتاجـها الطالب المترجم ، بل تحتوي على أبرزها فقط . وعلى الطالب أن يستعين بــالمعجم كلما رأى ذلك ضرورياً .

إضافة إلى النص باللغة المصدر والكلمات المساعدة ، تحـتوي كـل وحدة على تمرين لغوي ذي صلة بالنص . وأشيع هذه التمارين هنا هو تمرين الاشتقاق ، حيث تظهر عدة كلمات وردتْ في النص . وهي مصنفة إلى أفعال أو أسماء أو صفات ، وعلى الطالب أن يشتق النوعين الآخرين . مثـلاً ، إذا كانت الكلمة فعلاً ، فعليه أن يشتق منها الاسم والصفة . وإذا كانت صفـة ، فعليه ، أن يشتق منها الفعل والاسم ، وهكذا . وعليه أيضاً أن يكتـب المقـابل باللغة الأخرى أمام كل كلمة . والغاية من هذا التمرين إثراء حصيلة الطالب المفرداتية التي هي عامل أساسي في القدرة الترجمية .

وبما أن النصوص مقتبسة من كتب أو مجلات متنوعة ، فلقد ظـــهرت في آخر الكتاب قائمة تبين مصادر هذه الاقتباسات .

وختاماً ، أرجو أن يكون هذا الكتاب ذا فائدة لطلاب الترجمة ولكل مَنْ له اهتمام بالترجمة .

والحمد لله رب العالمين

أ.د. محمد علي الخولي

GENERAL PRINCIPLES OF
TRANSLATION

مبادئ عامة في الترجمة

في بداية هذا الكتاب ، يحسن تعريف الطالب بأهم المبادئ التي يجب أن تراعى في أثناء عملية الترجمة . ومن هذه المبادئ ما يلي:

1. إذا كانت الجملة في اللغة المصدر Source Language غامضة المعنى (أي متعددة المعاني لسبب نحوي أو سبب مفرداتي) ، فعلى المترجم أن يحاول إزالة غموضها في اللغة الهدف target language كلما أمكنه ذلك .

2. يستحسن أن ينقل المترجم التأثير الذي قصده الكاتب في اللغة المصدر إذا كان المترجم مدركاً لذلك التأثير . هل كان الكاتب ساخطاً أم ساخراً أم هازئاً أم غاضباً أم منفعلاً ... الخ ؟ وهذا لا يتأتى إلا بالممارسة والخبرة والدراية باللغتين (اللغة المصدر واللغة الهدف) .

3. لا بد للمترجم من أن يفهم النص تماماً كشرط مسبق للبدء في الترجمة ، إذ لا فائدة من ترجمة مبنية على سوء فهم النص .

4. على المترجم أن يتقيد بالمصطلحات المستخدمة في اللغة الهدف . وتزداد أهمية هذا المبدأ في الترجمة التخصصية ، أي ترجمة النصوص

المتخصصة في العلوم أو القانون أو سواها من فروع المعرفة . هنا لا يفيـد اختراع مصطلحات جديدة ، لا بد من الالتزام بالمصطلحــات الشائعـة
في اللغة الهدف لتحقيق التفاهم اللغوي المنشود .

5. الأصل في الترجمة هو التقيد بنص المصدر ، وهذا مــا يدعــى الترجمة الحرفية . وإذا تعذر ذلك لسبب ما ، فعلى المترجم أن يتحـول إلـى ترجمة المعنـى .

6. على المترجم الالتزام لترجمة ثابتة لمصطلح ما . فـإذا ترجـم المترجم المصطلح س بالمقابل ص في جملة ما في نص ما ، فعليـه أن يستخدم ص مقابل س كلما ظهرت س في اللغة المصدر من أجل تحقيق مبادئ الوضوح والثبات والاتساق consistency .

7. العدد الرقمي (3000 مثلاً) يترجم بعدد رقمي (3000) . والعدد الكتابي يترجم بعدد كتابي ، مثلاً three hundred تترجم بـ ثلاث مئة .

8. في بعض الحالات ، أو مصطلح يبقى كما هو . مثلاً ، phoneme يمكن أن تبقى كما هي (فونيم) ، fax تبقى (فاكس) .

9. الكلمة أو العبارة البارزة في اللغة المصدر يحافظ على بروزها في اللغة الهدف بطريقة مناسبة . مثلاً الكلمات المائلة أو المكتوبة بحرف أسود في اللغة المصدر يمكن إبرازها بالطريقة ذاتها أو بوضع خط تحتها في اللغة الهدف . عنوان الكتاب المكتوب بحرف مائل في اللغة الإنجليزية يترجم إلى العربية ويوضع تحته خط أو يطبع بحرف مائل .

10. قبل البدء بترجمة أول جملة في النص ، من الأفضــل أن يقـرأ المترجم النص كله كي يأخذ فكرة عامة عن الموضوع مما يسهل عليه ترجمة أجزائه .

11. كلمات النص نوعان : كلمات محتوى content words وكلمات وظيفية function words. على المترجم أن يترجم كلمــات المحــتوى ، ولكن ليس مطلوباً منه أن يترجم الكلمات الوظيفية ترجمة مباشرة دائمـاً لأن دور الكلمات الوظيفية يختلف عن دور الكلمات المحتوى . ومن أمثلة الكلمات الوظيفية to, a, an ,the, .

12. إذا أراد المترجم إضافة كلمة من عنده إلى النص الأصلي فعليه أن يضعها بين قوسين هكذا [   ] . مثلاً ، هناك أنواع عديدة [من البكتيريا] تعيش في جسم الإنسان . الإضافة التي بين قوسين يضيفهما المــترجم مــن أجل مزيد من التوضيح أو لإزالة الغموض حسبما يرى المــترجم الأمــر ضرورياً .

13. إذا أراد المترجم توضيح النص بإضافة طويلة أو التعليــق علــى النص ، فعليه أن يضيف ملاحظة هامشية footnote وألّا يضيــف ذلــك داخل النص ذلك . الإضافة داخل النص ذاته بين قوسين [   ] تقتصر على إضافة محدودة جداً لا تزيد عن كلمة أو اثنتين .

14.إذا كانت في اللغة الهدف عدة مقابلات لمصطلح مــا فــي اللغــة المصدر ، تعطى الأفضلية للأشيع أو الأدقّ منها .

15. بعد الترجمة الأولية , على المترجم أن يراجع النص للتأكد مــن سلامته من حيث النحو والإملاء والترقيم ولتخليص النص من أيــة ركاكــة أسلوبية محتملة .

16.لا يجوز للمترجم أن يخــترع من عنده اختصارات (كلمــات أوائلية) acronyms غــير مألوفــة لأن ذلــك يعيــق الاتصــال بيــن المترجم والقارئ . ولكن يجوز للمترجم في حالات محدودة أن يســتحدث اختصاراً بعد توضيحه اقتصاداً في التعبير إذا تكرر ظهور المصطلح عــدة مرات ، مثلاً م ج ع (ميثاق الجامعة العربية) .

17.إذا ظهرت كلمات أوائلية في اللغة المصدر ، فعلى المترجم أن يحولها إلى كلمات تامة في اللغة الهدف . مثلاً ، V I P تترجم إلى (شخص مهم جداً) ، N A T O تترجم إلى (منظمة معاهدة شمال الأطلسي) . وإذا كان الاختصار شائعاً جداً (مثل AIDS) ، فلا داعي لترجمته ، بل يمكن أن يبقى كما هو في اللغة المصدر (أي الإيدز) . ويجوز في بعض الحالات الجمع بين الاختصار وترجمته ، مثل النيتــو (منظمة معاهدة شمال الأطلسي) .

18. يحافظ المترجم على حدود الفقرات وعددها . أي تبدأ الفقرة فــي اللغة الهدف مع بداية الفقرة في اللغة المصدر وتنتهي مع نهايتها . وبذلــك ، تتطابق الفقرات في اللغة المصدر واللغة الهدف من حيث البدايــة والنهاية والعدد .

19. من حيث الترقيم الخارجي ، ويجب أن يتطابق النصان (في اللغة المصدر واللغة الهدف) في ترقيم أواخر الجمل . النقطة تبقى نقطة ، وكذلك علامة الاستفهام وعلامة التعجب وعلامات الاقتباس والفاصلة المنقوطة ، مع فروق طفيفة في شكل العلامة أحياناً . مثلاً ، في اللغة الإنجليزية نستعمل ؟ و ؛ وفي العربية نستعمل ؟ و ؛ . لاحظ أن المقصود بالترقيم الخارجي هو الترقيم في نهاية الجملة .

20. من حيث الترقيم الداخلي (أي الترقيم داخل الجملة وليس في نهايتها) ، قد تختلف اللغات في أحكام هذا الترقيم . مثلاً ، استخدام الفاصلة في اللغة العربية لا يتطابق مع استخدامها في اللغة الإنجليزية .

21. من حيث ترقيم الكلام المباشر ، نستخدم النقطتين في العربية والفاصلة في الإنجليزية . مثلاً ، قال : " ... " ، «... ». He said, . كما أن اتجاه علامات الاقتباس الفاتحة يختلف في اللغتين : نبدأ بـ " في الإنجليزية ، ولكن نبدأ بـ " في العربية . وكذلك ، تختلف علامات الاقتباس الخاتمة .

22. في العادة ، الاسم العَلَم لا يُترجم . مثلاً ، مُحَمَّد تبقى Muhammad ولا يجوز ترجمتها إلى the praised ، peter تصبح بيتر أو بطرس وليس (الصخرة) . أما إذا كان العلم اسماً جغرافياً مركباً فالأشيع ترجمته . مثلاً ، the Pacific Ocean تصبح (المحيط الهادي) ، the Red Sea تصبح (البحر الأحمر) .

23. على المترجم أن يرجع إلى المعاجم المتخصصة إذا كان يترجم نصاً متخصصاً ، مثلاً ، نصاً طبياً أو هندسياً أو قانونياً ، لأن المعاجم العامة في العادة لا تسعفه في الترجمة المتخصصة . المعجم العام يفيد في ترجمة النصوص العامة . وهناك معاجم متخصصة في شتى فروع العلوم والمعارف . هناك معاجم متخصصة عربية إنجليزية و إنجليزية عربية في الفيزياء والرياضيات والكيمياء والأحياء والتربية وعلم النفس والفلسفة وعلم اللغة والمحاسبة والإدارة والقانون والسياسة والحاسوب وكل فروع العلم ، بل إنّ هناك معاجم متخصصة في فروع الفروع ، من مثل علم اللغة النظري وعلم اللغة التطبيقي وعلم الأصوات .

24. على المترجم أن يتحرى الدقة في الترجمة وخاصة في ترجمة المصطلحات المتقاربة ، أي المصطلحات التي يتقارب معناها دون أن يتطابق.

25. على المترجم ألا يخمن معنى كلمة لا يعرفها دون الرجوع إلى المعجم ، إلاّ إذا كان في موقف ترجمة فورية أو ترجمة تتابعية . في هـــذه الحالة ، لا يوجد خيار آخر أمامه سوى خيار التخمين . و لكن ، إذا كان فـــي موقف ترجمة كتابية، فلا عذر له إذا لم يرجع إلى المعجــم للتثبت مـــن المعنى.

26. المعاني في أية لغة أكثر من الكلمات ، ولذلك يندر أن نجد كلمـــة ذات معنى واحد . معظم الكلمات متعددة المعاني . ومن واجب المـــترجم أن يفهم المعنى المقصود في اللغة المصدر كي يختار ما يقابله في اللغة الهدف .

وهذا هو التحدي الأكبر في عملية الترجمة: فهم النص في اللغة المصدر و إنشاء نص مقابل في اللغة الهدف.

27. الترجمة الكاملة ممكنة أحياناً ، ولكن الترجمة المُرْضية ممكنة دائماً ، إلاّ أنها تتطلب الدقة و الدراية و الخبرة.

28. النثر يترجم إلى نثر . أما الشعر فيجوز أن يترجم إلا شعر إن أمكن أو إلى نثر إذا تعذرت ترجمته إلى شعر.

29. يتوجب على المترجم أن يتقن اللغتين : اللغة المصدر و اللغة الهدف . يتقن الأولى ليفهم النص ويتقن الثانية ليكتب بها . ومن الواضح أن عدم الإتقان للأولى سيجعل الفهم مختلاً وأن عدم الإتقان للثانية سيجعل الكتابة مليئة بالأخطاء من كل نوع . وتصل الأمور إلى حد الكارثة إذا كان المترجم ضعيفاً في اللغتين : هنا تنشأ أخطاء عديدة في فهم اللغة المصدر وأخطاء عديدة في التعبير باللغة الهدف .

30. في الترجمة المتخصصة ، مثل الترجمة الطبية والهندسية ، يكون المترجم في وضع أفضل إذا كان عارفاً بالحقل الذي يترجم فيه ، بالإضافة إلى إتقانه للغتين بطبيعة الحال . ويمكن أن ندعو المعرفة بـالحقل المعرفة التخصصية و أن ندعو معرفة اللغتين المعرفة اللغوية . ومن الواضح أن المعرفة التخصصية لا تغني عن المعرفة اللغوية , فالمعرفة الطبية ، مثـــلاً ، لا تجعل الطبيب مترجماً . ولكن ، قد تغني المعرفة اللغوية عن المعرفة التخصصية ، إذ يـستطيع المترجم أن يـترجم نصـاً طبيـاً دون أن يكـون متخصصاً في الطب . ولا شك أن خير المترجمين من كـانت تتوفر لديـه .

المعرفة التخصصية والمعرفة اللغوية معاً ، ولكن قليلاً بل نادراً ما يتوفر مثل هؤلاء المترجمين .

31. إن عملية الترجمة اتخاذ قرارات في كل لحظة ، إذ لا بد أن يتخذ المترجم قراراً عند ترجمة كل كلمة وعند ترجمة كل تركيب .   وبالطبع ، حسن اتخاذ القرار يعتمد أساساً على المقدرة اللغوية للمترجم وعلى درايته بفن الترجمة أو علم الترجمة . كما أن عملية الترجمة - في العديد من المواقف - عملية تستدعي إعادة المحاولة ، أي الترجمة إلــى الأمــام ثـم العودة إلى الخلف ثم إلى الأمام ، حتى يحسّ المترجم أن المنتوج قد اسـتوى و استقرّ و أصبح مُرضياً من حيث المعنى والمبنى .

32. للطالب العربي ، الترجمة من الإنجليزية إلى العربية أسهل بكثير من الترجمة من العربية إلى الإنجليزية ، لأن الترجمة من الإنجليزية تستدعي فـهم الإنجليزية والتعبير بالعربية ، ولكنّ الترجمة من العربية تستدعي فهم العربية والتعبير بالإنجليزية . صعوبة الأولى فهم الإنجليزية ، أما صعوبــة الثانية فهي التعبير بالإنجليزية . و لا شك أن التعبير أصعب من الفهم ، فـي أغلب الأحيان .

UNIT 1

LEARNING AND ACQUIRING

There are a few questions which have occupied language teachers for centuries and probably always will. Of these perhaps the most basic is 'How does a person come to control a language anyway?' We all achieved this feat with our first language, and many of us have gained some ability in other language by studying them in school. The term 'acquisition' is sometimes used for the former, and 'learning' for what goes on in the classroom. There has been considerable discussion about whether these two processes are essentially the same, or essentially the same, or essen- tially different. Unit very recently, however, people have gener- ally assumed that one followed the other with perhaps a few years' overlap. The ability to 'acquire' supposedly died out at about the age of puberty, while 'learning' became possible only in the early school years as the necessary 'readiness's' developed.

More recently , though, some research has indicated that the picture is not quite like that. It my be that the same kind of acquisition we see in children can continue well into adulthood – perhaps throughout life. Or it may be that what some people call 'adult acquisition' is really a third process. Be that as it may, however, it is becoming clear that adults and adolescents do have available to them at least two modes of gaining control of a new language.

The better known of these two modes is (in a special, narrowed sense) called 'learning.' Here, learning .' begins with selection of some clearly defined element which is to be learned. In helping someone else to learn, your job is to teach (again in a specially restricted sense of that word). In teaching, you first present the new item as clearly and interestingly as you can. Then you have your students practice the item in one way or another until they seem to have got it. When the time comes, you go on to test them on it. Finally, you may or may not get around to using it with them in some communicative way.

In this kind of teaching and learning, then, the very act of selecting an item pulls it out of the context of normal com- municative exchange. To compensate for this severing of the normal interrelationship you may go to some length to provide context as you present, drill and test it.

In acquisition, the person who is doing the acquiring meets words in the full context of some kind of genuine human communication. There is no special presentation of a new item, no organized drilling, and no testing in the academic sense. Conversation is about things which the acquirer understands and which are already clear in his mind. Because a teacher cannot read minds, this requirement commonly means that in the beginning most of the conversation will be about what is present in the classroom at the time. The language used is generally at a level which the acquirer already controls or a little beyond that level. The acquirer follows the discourse comfort-ably, drawing on context to fill in the meanings of new words and constructions. In time he becomes able to produce new items correctly, but for a while he may remain largely silent. When he does speak, those around him react in terms of their attempts to communicate, and not in terms of the correctness or incorrectness, and not in terms of the correctness or incorrectness of what he has said.

This kind of acquisition takes time and patience. Until a student has acquired an item, he will make numerous errors in its use. Learning by contrast, produces correct forms almost immediately.

There are however some weighty advantages to acquisition as compared with learned may forgot- ten after (or before !) the next test, while what has been acquired is relatively permanent. What has been acquired serves directly as the basis for smooth production either of speech or of writing. Learned material is useful for monitoring, correcting or translating what has originated from material which has already been acquired either in the target language or in the native language, *but not for much else.* Not least, learning will work only for those items which can be stated fairly simply: English *house* corresponds to Spanish *casa*, for example, and the ending-s is used only for English verbs which are in the present tense with a third person singular subject. Acquisition works for everything; for all of the matters that i' ve just mentioned. but also for phonetic nuances, use of definite and indefinite articles, choice of just the right preposition or verb tense, and so on. The essential difference between learning and acquisition may lie in what the student does with what is put in front of him, but many parts of a language simply defy anyone to perform learning on them!

Over the centuries language teachers have used countless methods and rechniques. Most of the time, by whatever method, we have concentrated on trying to teach so that our students would learn. Acquisition has come- when it has come at all-as a desirable but incidental by-product of good teaching and good learning. Its recent identification as a separate process casts light on what we have been doing all along.

Helpful Vocabulary :

learning and acquiring   التعلم والاكتساب

to gain ability   يحصل على قدرة

considerable discussion   جدل كبير

essentially the same   متماثلان بشكل أساسي

until very recently   حتى وقت قريب

one followed the other   أحدهما تَبَعَ الآخر

age of puberty   سِنّ البلوغ

indicated that   دَلَّ على أنَّ

perhaps throughout life   ربَّما طيلة الحياة

it may be that   من المحتمل أنَّ

adult acquisition   اكتسأب البلوغ

be that as it may   ومهما يكن من أمر

the very act of selecting   فِعلُ الاختيار ذاتُه

communicative exchange   تبادل اتصالي

present, drill, test   يعْرِض ، يدرِّب ، يختبر

special presentation   عَرْض خاص

in the academic sense   بالمعنى الأكاديمي

a little beyond that level   أعلى قليلاً من ذلك المستوى

in time   في الوقت المناسب

for a while   لفترة وجيزة ، لبُرْهةٍ

by contrast   بالمقارنة

as compared with   عند مقارنتها بـِ

Exercise 1. *Translate the previous passage into Arabic.*

Exercise 2. *Fill in this table with the suitable English derivatives whenever possible, and write down the Arabic equivalents of all the words.*

Verb		Noun		Adjective	
English	**Arabic**	**English**	**Arabic**	**English**	**Arabic**
forget					
		question			
occupy					
control					
gain					
learn					
		process			
				Available	
acquire					
		adult			
				normal	
indicate					
restrict					
		test			
		communication			
				genuine	
assume					
		language			

Exercise 3. *Translate these words related to the same filed :*

learn	_____	instruct	_____
teach	_____	instructor	_____
learner	_____ instruction	تدريس	
teacher	_____ teaching	تعليم	

UNIT 2

ENGLAND AND SHAKESPEAR

T HE winds that scattered the Spanish Armada blew English litera- ture, which had been merely smouldering for generations, into a blaze of genius, Elizabeth, who was to give her name to this glorious outburst, had in fact reigned for thirty years before it arrived, and most of its supreme achievements in poetic drama and in prose argument came in the reign of her successor, James the First. Neverthe- less, we are right to call this great ago of literature 'Elizabethan',for its greatness belongs in spirit to that strange indomitable indomitable Queen, just as its decadence later seems to share the stifling atmosphere of James's court. And clearly there are two questions about this Elizabethan age we must ask and try to answer. Why did it arrive so late, after the Queen herself had been reigning for thirty years, long after the Renaissance in Italy and France hade come to an end come to an end? And why, when it did arrive, when the sixteenth century had only twelve more years to run, should it suddenly break into that firework display of poetic genius?

The first question is easily answered. Great literature demands a language that is at once a powerful and very flexible instrument an organ with more than one keyboard and many stops. This instrument was not ready; the organ was only being assembled. English literary forms were either borrowed from Italy and France, as in much of the verse of Surrey and Wyatt, or, as with the prose-men, also often busy with translation, were still crudely experimenting with syntax, with the first creaky wooden machinery of prose style. Nor is this surprising. The England of the Tudors was a new country, even though in some respects it was more medieval and traditional than most of Southern Europe; and it was a new country out on the edge of things, as yet away from the main stream of civilization. Its famous long- bows had been made obsolete by gunpowder; it had a militia but no real army; it had plenty of ships, boldly exploring, trading and privateering, but as yet they hardly constituted a navy. True. Its wealth was rapidly increasing, London. was growing fast; its new social order, created by Henry the Eighth and confirmed and stabilised by the adroit Elizabeth, was proving effective and a source of new energy, and the nationalism of the age, nothing strange to these islanders, was triumphant and irresistible here. But too much was happening all at once; enormous effort was required, as nobody knew better than Elizabeth herself, to cope with every immediate situation. So those first thirty years of her reign were years of effort, of solemn endeavour. Of will and purpose, all reflected in the writing of the time, in the didactic prose work of Ascham and Elyot, even in the little that was done by the splendid Sidney in the earlier poetry of the great Spenser. Then came the threat of the Spanish Armada, crammed with the dreaded infantrymen of Spain; the ultimate challenge. The challenge was met, the Armada defeated and, the very elements being on England's side (as they ought to be, in English opinion), finally destroyed; the great black shadow of Spain suddenly vanished; Elizabethan England had come through where the sun was out and the bells were ringing.

This explains the sudden release of release of energy, the nation in flower. But it it does not provide a complete answer to our second question- why this flowering should reach, in a few years, such a dazzling height of poetic genius. Perhaps a complete answer cannot be found, the *zeitgeist*, then as now, having too many secret operations. But some contribu- tions towards it are possible. First, the energy was there, ready to be released into art. Next, this was a nation highly conscious of itself as a nation; a late Elizabethan, a subject of the magnificent old Queen, was very much an Elizabethan. Now to this release of energy and this national self-consciousness we must add a third factor. Within the national unity of this comparatively small society there was astonish-ing variety; it contained, for example not only Anglicans but also Catholics, puritans, skeptics and atheists. It was grimly ascetic and wildly licentious; it reached extremes of brutality and refinement, and a building that offered bear-baiting on Wednesday would be playing Romeo and Juliet on Thursday. A merchant might invest his money in wool or in a search for El Dorado; good advice might be sought from Francis Bacon, the father of scientific method. or Dr. Dee, the necro- mancer; capitalism in a black sit rubbed elbows with the velvet or rags of dying feudalism; the great Queen's court seemed equidistant between the Tower, with its thumbscrews and scaffolds, and fairyland. The life of this London was an incredible medley of lutes and lice, silks and ordure, madrigals and the plague, industrious apprentices and pimps and harlots, white-faced puritan preachers and red-faced drunken poets. During this brief period, each class had something almost theatrical about it, appeared to be over-playing its part: the great nobles moved in an unending pageant, and the lesser sold estates to buy a suit and three sets of livery for possible appearances at Court; the new middle class counted its money, donned clean linen to listen to sermons, ate beef and pudding, locked up its daughters, all suddenly and tremendously bourgeois; the common folk, the crowd, the mob, shook its fists or threw up its caps, rioted or rollicked, like the chorus in an opera. To this ago, we feel, everything was titanic.

Helpful Vocabulary :

blaze of genius	وَهَجَ من العبقرية
poetic drama	المسرحية الشعرية
supreme achievements	إنجازات رائعة
reign of her successor	حُكْم خليفتها
age of literature	عَصْر الأدب
stifling atmosphere	جَو خانِق
as in much of	كما في كثير من
prose-men	رجال النثر، ناثرون
prose style	الأسلوب النثري
in some respects	في بعض النواحي
nationalism of the age	قومية العصر
didactic prose	نثر تعليمي
in the little that	في القليل الذي
the ultimate challenge	التحدي النهائي
release of energy	انطلاق الطاقة
highly conscious of itself	مدركة جداً لنفسها
poetic genius	عبقرية شعرية
capitalism and feudalism	الرأسمالية والإقطاعية
new middle class	الطبقة الوسطى الجديدة
to this age	بالنسبة لهذا العصر
moral order	نظام أخلاقي
brutality and refinement	القسوة والتهذيب

Exercise 1 . *Translate the previous passage into Arabic.*

Exercise 2. *Fill in this table with the suitable English derivatives whenever possible, and write down the Arabic equivalents of all the words.*

Verb		Noun		Adjective	
English	**Arabic**	**English**	**Arabic**	**English**	**Arabic**
arrive					
		genius			
answer					
		successor			
				poetic	
end					
		queen			
try					
		year			
				great	
demand					
		instrument			
stabilize					
		syntax			
				triumphant	
		challenge			
				strange	
				immediate	

Exercise 3. *Translate this group of words related to the same semantic field :*

drama	_____	song	_____
dramatist	_____	novel	_____
play	_____	novelist	_____
sonnet	_____	poet	_____
poem	_____	eulogy	_____

UNIT 3

WHAT IS LITERATURE, And WHY DO WE STUDY IT?

We use the word **literature,** in a broad sense, to mean compositions that tell stories, dramatize situations, express emotions, and analyze and advocate ideas. Before the invention of writing, literary works were necessarily spoken or sung and were retained only as long as living people performed them. In some societies, the oral tradition of literature still exists, with many poems and stories designed exclusively for spoken delivery. Evan in our modern age of writing and printing, much literature is still heard aloud rather than read silently. Parents delight their children with stories and poems; poets and storywriters read their works directly before live audiences; and plays and scripts are interpreted on stages and before cameras for the benefit of a vast public.

No matter how we assimilate literature, we gain much from it. In truth, readers often cannot explain why they enjoy reading, for goals and ideals are not easily articulated. There are, however, areas of general agreement about the value of systematic and extensive reading.

Literature helps us grow, us grow, both personally and intellectually. It provides an objective base for knowledge and understanding. It links us with the broader cultural, philosophic, and religious world of which we are a part it enables us to recognize human dreams and struggles in different place and times we would never otherwise know existed. It helps us develop mature sensibility and compassion for the condition of all living things- human, animal, and vegetable. It gives us the knowledge and perception to appreciate the beauty of order and arrangement, just as a well- structured song or a beautifully painted canvas can. It provides the comparative basis from which we can see worthiness in the aims of all people, and it therefore helps us see beauty in the world around us. It exercises our emotions through interest, concern, tension, excitement, hope, fear, regret, laughter, and sym- pathy. Through our cumulative experience in reading, literature shapes our goals and values by clarifying our own identities- both positively through acceptance of the admirable in human beings, and negatively, through refection of the sinister. It enables us to develop a perspective on events occurring locally and globally, and thereby it give us understanding and control. It encourages us to assist creative, talented people who need recognition and support. It is one of the shaping influence of life. Literature makes us human.

TYPES OF LITERATURE: THE GENRES

Literature may be classified into four categories or *genres*: (1) prose fiction, (2) poetry, (3) drama, and (4) nonfiction prose. Usually the first three are classed as **imaginative literature.**

The genres of imaginative literature have much in common. but they also have distinguishing characteristics. **Prose fiction**, or **narrative fiction** includes **myths, parables, romances, novels,** and **short stories.** Originally, *fiction* meant anything made up, crafted, or shaped, but today the word refers to prose stories based in the author's imagination. The essence of fiction is **narration**, the relating or recounting of a sequence of events or actions. Works of fiction usually focus of one or a few major characters who undergo a change of attitude or character as they interact with other characters and deal with problems. While fiction, like all imaginative literature, may introduce true historical details, it is not real history. Its main purpose is to interest, stim-ulate, instruct, and divert, not to create a precise historical record.

Poetry expresses a conversation or interchange that is grounded in the most deeply felt experiences of human beings. Poetry exists in many formal and informal shapes, from the brief haiku to the extensive **epic**. More eco- nomical than prose fiction in its use of words, poetry relies heavily on **imagery, figurative language**, and **sound.**

Drama is literature designed to be performed by actors. Like fiction, drama may focus on a single character or a single character or a small number of characters, and it enacts fictional events as if they were happening in the present, to be wit- nessed by an audience. Although most modern plays use prose dialogue, in the belief that dramatic speech should be as lifelike as possibly, many plays from the past, like those of ancient Greece and Renaissance England, are in poetic form.

Nonfiction prose is the literary genre that consists of news reports, fea- ture articles, essays, editorials, textbooks, historical and biographical and the like, all of which describe or interpret facts and present judgments and opinions. Major goals of nonfiction prose are to report truth and to pre-sent logic in reasoning. Whereas in imaginative literature the aim is it show truth in life and human nature, in nonfiction prose the goal is to reveal truth in the factual world of news, science, and history.

Helpful Vocabulary :

in a broad sense	بمعنى أوسع
literary works	أعمال أدبية
spoken delivery	إلقاء شفهي
live audience	مستمعون أحياء
no matter how	بغض النظر عن كيف
in truth	في الحقيقة
extensive reading	قراءة موسعة
personally and intellectually :	شخصياً و ذهنياً
objective base	قاعدة موضوعية
mature sensibility	إحساس ناضج
cumulative experience	خبرة تراكمية
perspective on events	وجهة نظر عن الأحداث
locally and globally	محلياً و علمياً
prose fiction	قصص نثري
nonfiction prose	نثر غير قصصي
imaginative literature	أدب خيالي
narrative fiction	خيال قصصي
extensive epic	ملحمة مطولة
figurative language	لغة مجازية
prose dialogue	حوار نثري
biographical works	أعمال السِّيَر
factual world	عالم الحقيقة

Exercise 1 . *Translate the previous passage into Arabic.*

Exercise 2. *Fill in this table with the suitable English derivatives whenever possible, and write down the Arabic equivalents of all the words.*

Verb		Noun		Adjective	
English	Arabic	English	Arabic	English	Arabic
dramatize					
express					
		benefit			
				broad	
analyze					
		parent			
				silent	
advocate					
enjoy					
				admirable	
articulate					
				local	
perceive					
		acceptance			
compare					
		shape			

Exercise 3. *Translate this group of words related to the   same field :*

silent reading

intensive reading

supplementary

oral reading

model reading

extensive reading

UNIT 4

ARABIA AND HER
NEIGHBOURS

T HE peninsula of Arabian may be described as a vast tectangle ofmore thanmillion square miles in extent, placed between Africa and the main land-mass of Asia. The Red Sea, which forms its western boundary, is part of the great rift vally which continues northwards through the Gulf of Akaba, the Dead Sea, and the River Jordan: the hug convulsions which produced it have piled up mountain ridges which rise steeply along the coast from the Hijaz to the Yemen, and the land thus slopes down from west to east towards the gentle declivity of the Persain Gulf. On three sides Arabia faces the sea; her only land frontier is the Syrian Desert and as the corssing of these sandy wastes was at least as difficult as landing on her almost harbourless coasts, the long remained an isolated and inaccessible country, whose inhabitants aptly styled her *Jazirat al- Arab*, the *island* of the Arabs.

The climate of Arabia is distinguished chiefly by high tempera- ture and the absence of moisture. The autumn monsoon deposits heavy showers on the coastline of Oman and the Yemen, but the steep hills force the rain- laden clouds to ascend rapidly and dis- charge their contents before they have passed over the inland slops; the winter and spring rains of the Mediterranean region are scattered sparsely over the northern deserts, the *Nufud*, where the wilderness blossoms like a rose for a short season, but the southern interior is beyond their range, and is in consequence a dreadful waterless waste, the Rub al- khali, the Empty Quarter, which until recent times has rarely been crossed by European travelers. Arabic is destitute of lades, forests and prairies; scarcely a perennial stream is found in the land: the *wadis* or rivers. Which become raging tor- rents in the short wet period, are for most of the year dry and emp- ty and a man might cross their beds without being aware of their existence. Except in the high country. The heat of the summer is in- tense, yet the climate is not on the whole injurious to human health the dryness of the atmosphere mitigates the strength of the sun's

Rays; the nights are cool; in winter snow often lies in the highest valleys of the Jabal Shammar, a chain of gills immediately south of the Nufud, and frost is not unknown not unknown in the highlands of the Yemen.

Western Arabia. the mountainous region fronting the Red Sea, consists of three clearly defined areas: a hot, narrow coastal plain. Known as the Tihama. Or lowland; hills, with peaks rising to several thousand feet, which bear the name of Hijaz, or barrier and beyond these, a great plateau which dips eastwards to the central deserts. In the north, the land of Midian, the mountains are wild and deso- late, but in the Yemen, the Arabia felix of the ancients, the hill- sides receive a substantial rainfall, and grain crops and (since the sixteenth century) the coffe bean are grown in the fertile valleys. Here, in the extreme south- west corner of the peninsula, arose the earliest civilizations of old Arabia, those of the Munaeans and Sabaeans. Southern Arabic presents an inhospitable front to the Indian Ocean; its long coastline has few natural harbours, and its inhabited valleys lie inland and free from prying strangers. Its prin- cipal division, the Hadramawt, was famous in remote antiquity as the land of incense; the gum from the incense- trees was a prized article of commerce, and vast quantities of it were bought and burnt on the altars of Egyptian and Babylonian temples. Easten Arabia is a land of contrasts. The shores of the Persian Gulf are flat, bar- ren and humid, the natives deriving a scanty living from fishing and pearl- diving, bit the province of Oman is filled with well- watered vales which run back to the foothills of the Jabal Akhdar, or Green Mountains, and whose palm-orchards support a substantial population. The interior of Arabia is by no means all desert; many oases provide food and water for consider-able settlements: springs and wells afford refreshment to the travel-ler and some large fertile depression, such as the Wadi Hadra- mawt in the south and the Wadi Sirhan in the north-west, have ser- ved for ages as channels of commerce.

The name 'Arab, which may possibly be connected with the Hebrew root, abhar, to move or pass, to move or pass, has been often restricted to the desert-dwellers. The *Badw* or Bedouins. And repudiated by the townsmen and peasants, a practice which reminds us that the majority of the inhabitants of the peninsula have since historic times been pastoral nomads. The pattern of their life has remained unchanged through the centuries since the days of Abraham.

Helpful Vocabulary :

the peninsula of Arabia	شبة الجزيرة العربية
In extent	مساحة ، من حيث الاتساع
Syrian desert	صحراء الشام
Sandy wastes	القفار الرملية
harbourless coasts	سواحل دون موانئ
isolated country	بلد منعزل
destitute of lakes	خالية من البحيرات
distinguished chiefly by	تتميز أساساً بـــ
absence of moisture	غياب الرطوبة
autumn monsoon	الرياح الموسمية الخريفية
rain-laden clouds	سحب محمّلة بالمطر
inland slopes	المنحدرات الداخلية
beyond their range	وراء مداها ، خارج مداها
The Empty Quarter	الرُّبع الخالي
Chain of hills	سلسلة تلال
mountainous region	منطقة جبلية
coastal plain	سهل ساحلي
central deserts	الصحارى الوسطى
in remote antiquity	في الماضي البعيد
land of incense	أرض البخور
Babylonian temples	معابد بابلية
Channels of commerce	خطوط التجارة ، ممرات للتجارة

Exercise 1 . *Translate the previous passage into Arabic.*

Exercise 2. *Fill in this table with the suitable English derivatives whenever possible, and write down the Arabic equivalents of all the words.*

Verb		Noun		Adjective	
English	**Arabic**	**English**	**Arabic**	**English**	**Arabic**
place					
		rectangle			
				difficult	
continue					
ascend					
		inhabitant			
travel					
		season			
				gentle	
blossom					
		style			
				heavy	
force					
		sand			
		hill			
grow					
		rage			
				dry	

Exercise 3. *Translate this group of words related to the same field :*

gulf	_____	shore	_____
range	_____	island	_____
mountain	_____	peninsula	_____
plain	_____	strait	_____
coast	_____	ocean	_____

UNIT 5

SOME INTELLECTUAL FOUATIONS OF POLITICAL SOCIOLOGY

IN THIS CHAPTER we shall set out and examine a number of different theories or perspective on the nature and working of social processes political sociologists place themselves within a number of traditions of thought which go back almost to the origins of self-conscious reflection about man and his social relationships. What we shall do in this chapter is to spell out some of the contributions these various traditions make to a discussion of the problem of order, a problem we thirik of as being central to the concern of political sociology. Briefly, what we understand by social order is that process whereby the interactions of members of social groups become patterned, that is to say the interactions are relatively stable over time and the form which they from time to time is relatively predict- able.

social order. The problem of endurance and change, has always been seen as problematic, as something that needs to be understood either for its own sake or because it was felt that enquiry was likely to lead to controlled change. Perhaps the major difference between Plato and Aristotle was concerned with detached observation. Whatever the case, it is certainly true that the problem of order is not necessarily one which is the sole concern of the more conservative-minded theorist. Social order can hardly be imagined without its opposite, social disorder, and any useful explana- tion of the one well contain, at least implicitly, an explanation of the other although, as in the cases of functional analysis and conflict theory, some theoretical perspectives are biased towards order and breakdown respec- tively. However, the traditional emphasis on order has a strong, if rather

imprecise, empirical content since it is 'obviously' true that most societies mcst of the time display order rather than chaos! If, then, we begin with the assumption of order we are not making a prescriptive judgement (lest the philosophical heavens fall) but we are simply beginning the discussion on the basis of a rather commonplace observation.

it is easy to explain why the concern with order has been a central question in the history of social though: if society is to persist for any length of time the people making up that society must live without undue threat or likelihood of death. Perhaps the tag line from Hobbes. familiar to all students of the history of ideas, that in the state of nature the life of man is 'solitary,brings, out this concept most vividly. The fact that the human frame is fragile and easily destroyed makes norms or laws prohibiting violence, except under special circum- stances, a necessity for any type of social order is almost certainly necessary so that social life may continue, in the sense that without it, people may reproduce, but they will not be able to train or induct children since there will be nothing into which they can be in-ducted; in other words, there would be no society. Although this is very little more than the most glaring of truisms, it is still true that the problem of producing and maintaining order is a real one. Order is not something that the social scientist can take as a 'given', the product, say, of man's biological or genetic make-up, and hence a problem for the biologist or biochemist but not for the sociologist. It is. To repeat ourselves, problem-atic in at least the practical sense that all societies at some time display symptoms of a breakdown of order.

Broadly speaking, social thought has suggested three lines of attack on the problem of order which we shall present in a slightly abbreviated and exaggerated from in order to isolate the main themes of the three argu-ments. We shall also attempt to outline the defects and strength of each perspective and outline the kind of image of man and society upon which they are founded. We shall investigate the intellectual problem areas connected with each of these three perspective that have been brought out by the various proponents. Coercion theories of one sort or another have from the beginning of systematic thinking about society stressed the primacy of force as the agency underlying social order and obedience. Secondly, society has been envisaged as some sort of mutual interest organization within which a sensible or rational (that is in terms of calcu-lating) appraisal of the casts and benefits of social actions lead men to remain peaceful members of society. Equally venerable is the tradition that argues the priority of some sort of popular commitment to the norms or goals of the state or society.

Helpful Vocabulary :

social processes	عمليات اجتماعية
Political sociologists	علماء الاجتماع السياسي
Problem of order	مشكلة النظام
stable over time	مستقرة على مدى الزمن
relatively predictable	قابل للتنبؤ نسبياً
controlled change	تغيُّر مُسَيطَرٌ عليه
whatever the case	مهما تكن الحالة
sole concern	الاهتمام الوحيد
social disorder	فوضى اجتماعية
at least implicitly	على الأقل ضمناً
functional analysis	تحليل وظيفي
conflict theory	نظرية الصراع
respectively	على التوالي
prescriptive judgment	حُكم فَرْضي ، حكم معياري
social thought	فِكُر اجتماعي
breakdown of order	تصدع النظام
in the practical sense	بالمعنى العلمي
genetic make-up	التكوين الوراثي
in the sense that	بمعنى أنَّ
popular commitment	التزام شعبي
norms of the society	مُثُل المجتمع

Exercise 1 . *Translate the previous passage into Arabic.*

Exercise 2. *Fill in this table with the suitable English derivatives whenever possible, and write down the Arabic equivalents of all the words.*

Verb		Noun		Adjective	
English	**Arabic**	**English**	**Arabic**	**English**	**Arabic**
examine					
				different	
				conscious	
		conflict			
				brief	
found					
		bias			
				central	
				relative	
attempt					
		norm			
				necessary	
calculate					
		man			
				popular	
		concept			
display					

Exercise 3. *Translate this group of words related to the same field :*

Psychology _____ methodology _____

sociology _____ biology _____

anthropology _____ zoology _____

politics _____ botany _____

UNIT 6

GAMES AND LANGUAGE TEACHING

There are hundreds of games that can be used in some connection with language teaching. In this book we shall be looking at ways in which they can be integrated with teaching so that they be-come a positive part of it rather than a time-filler or, worse, a time-waster.

An effective user of games in the language classroom is not necessarily the teacher who has a long list of them in his head, but
someone who has really thought about them and knows their ingredients and how they can be varied to cal l forth different activities and skills from the players. A teacher who understands games in this way is much more likely to be able to find or create games that will help his students to learn something as they play.

The most obvious way of classifying games from a language they prac-tise: listening games, spelling games, games to help students build vocabulary, games that bring in a structure or a function and so on. Figure 1 groups some of the games mentioned in this book under headings like this.

Looking at the language skills involved is a good start when considering whether a particular game will be suitable for a particular purpose, but other features may be just as important Does the game need the teacher or someone else to act as leader or master of ceremonies, for example, or can it be played by groups of students on their own ? Are the players competing, and, if so, in teams or individually, or is it a game in which players can co-operate ? Is it an active noisy game or one which can be played quietly sitting at desks? These and other factors make different games practically as well as pedagogically suitable for different circumstances.

But, first of all, what is a game? How do games and learning fit together? Looking at games in general, with examples from the everyday world well as from games specially designed with teaching in mind, may help us to pick out features that will be useful in language teaching and to see what other features will be less useful or even a waste of time.

A game consists of play governed by rules. Kicking a ball around in the park is play : adding rules about how and were you can kick the ball and giving your efforts an objective (like getting it between two goalposts) turn this play into a game. This is summed up very well in Gibbs' definition (1978 : P. 60) of a game as ' an activity carried out by cooperating or competing decision-makers, seeking to achieve, within a set of rules, their object-tives'. Applying this to teaching, one can see how students play-ing a game are encouraged to use language to some purpose. The purpose may be an artificial one determined by the game, but the skills exercised to achieve that purpose may be applied in everyday life just like the skills used in 'ordinary' games. These are many and varied : coordination of hand and eye in games like netball and tennis, memory in a game like pelmanism, tactics in draughts or chess. Whatever the game, the skills employed in it are developed and improved through the repeated use they get, and, most important, the players want to improve the skills necessary for a game they enjoy. Both these principles apply to language games too.

For language- teaching purposes we need to make sure that the skills needed in any game are heavily enough weighted on the language side. For example, chess is an excellent game in itself, but it is almost useless from the language-teaching point of view. The obvious reason is that players need not communicate with one another during the game- at least not with words. The skill used in chess are intellectual and tactical and not linguistic. This

Helpful Vocabulary :

in some connection with	فيما يتصل بـــ
language teaching	تعليم اللغة
integrated with	متكاملة مع
so that they become	بحيث تصبح
effective user	مستخدِم فعَّال
way of classifying	طريقة لتصنيف
his point of view	وجهة نظره
listening games	ألعاب الاستماع
spelling games	العاب التهجئة
language skills	مهارات لغوية
pedagogically suitable	ملائم تربوياً
fit together	تتلاءَم معاً
with teaching in mind	مع استهداف التعليم
play governed by rules	لَعِبٌ محكوم بقوانين
competing decision-makers	صانعو القرار المتنافسون
artificial purpose	هدف مُصطنَع
many and varied	كثيرة ومتنوعة
coordination of hand and eye	تناسق اليد والعين
language- teaching purposes	أهداف تعليم اللغة
weighted on the language side	تميل إلى جانب اللغة
intellectual skill	مهارة ذهنية
considerable adaptation	تعديل كبير

Exercise 1 . *Translate the previous passage into Arabic.*

Exercise 2. *Fill in this table with the suitable English derivatives whenever possible, and write down the Arabic equivalents of all the words.*

Verb		Noun		Adjective	
English	Arabic	English	Arabic	English	Arabic
		connection			
				integrated	
				positive	
play					
				necessary	
spell					
involve					
				suitable	
				noisy	
		ceremony			
				particular	
		purpose			
encourage					
cooperate					
				artificial	
govern					
				excellent	
repeat					

Exercise 3. *Translate these abbreviations :*

TEFL	تعليم الإنجليزية كلغة أجنبية	TOEFL	_____
TESL	_____	LI	_____
TENL	_____	L2	
TESOL	تعليم الإنجليزية لمتكلمي اللغات الأخرى	FL	_____
FLT	_____	SL	_____

UNIT 7

CHANGES IN GEOGRAPHY TEACHING

The scientific attempt to understand the geography of the world is less than a century old. It is not surprising that geography should have evolved and developed as people spread over the world and took possession of its various parts. Since these times. The world has changed as well as the educational milieu in which geography is taught.

Changes in the teaching environment

A century ago. the teaching of geography was aidea by wall maps: photographs were not normaily available. Thirty years ago audio- visual aids. Including a erial photographs and television. Were in their infancy. Today potential resources seem almost unlimited in number from census data to computerized data banks, from maps to various visual illustrations. Such as a erial photography from remote sensing equipment (see Fig. 7.2). At the present time we can look at photographs which show us the earth as a whole without needing the mediation of a cartographer. We are now. therefore. much more familiar with such view of the earth. from which results a new relationships between man and his planer. whether or not he is conscious of this. to see the earth as a whole. to see it daily being transformed. change in colour in a way that one is used to seeing the moon, will be events as familiar to the pupils of tomorrow as is today their view of the street outside their home; all this owing to satellite photography.

Changes in the students

The students and pupils of today live in a cultural context very different from that of 20 years ago. let alone 50 years ago. School. the teacher. the textbook and teaching aids are no longer the only sources of information: numerous channels of information are available and used outside the school: magazines and newspapers. radio, television. All bombard the students each day with a mass of

Information, to such an extent that sometimes their reaction is to   reject it. Such information consists either of descriptions of events which have been consciously or unwittingly or unwittingly distorted, or of interpret- tation of these events containing value judgements. Such interpreta-tions clearly mediate the reality that the reader or viewer would have perceived and judged. It is therefore necessary to teach the young to examine such information critically. To get them to sort out facts from opinion, which can only be done through their having a wide cognitive perspective.

But students. the world over, have an unequal experience of space and spatial relations. Millions of children have never seen the sea, a mountain . a cliff, a glacier. a skyscraper or farm. In adult life. however, many young people will experience varied environments. for example the rural and urban landscapes experi-enced by migrants. Visits to relations in other parts of the world. Holidays, school journeys, travel grants- all are now faceletating the acquisition of knowledge about a world which is becoming more and more accessible for some students. Yet. It is still true that a gulf is growing between the vicarious experience of the world made possible by the mass media and direct experience made possible by travel. further, such direct contact with distant parts is becoming more discontinuous. Because it is possible to fly from once place to another rapidly, personal knowledge of places separated by long distances may be better than knowledge of intervening areas. Including areas close to one's home. Direct experience of the world is also made unequal by income difference. whether these be on a national scale or at the individual scale within a nation.

Geographical education must be seen. Therefore, as an integral part of the process of education, since such an education must make the student better able to understand life on earth by making evident spatial relations and the organization of space by man. Geographical education cannot be limited to those who in some form or other hope to practice geography professionally. It seems normal to us that all children should learn to read. to write. To count and calculate, that is to acquire the means of communicating with others, so that they may ask questions and give answers, that they may listen and also be heard, so that they may cope with daily life, so that they may exploit their aptitudes and develop their personalities. Is it less natural that students should learn to operate competently in space. To develop the habit of looking at the spatial aspects of problems. In order that they may better understand the environments in which they live?

Changes in geographical knowledge

A little more than a century ago. men were still exploring the coasts of certain continents and wondering about the possible existence of an Antarctic land mass. The interiors of Africa. Australia and south America were little known to geographers.

Helpful Vocabulary :

not normally available	ليست متوفرة عادة
audio-visual aids	وسائل سمعية وبصرية
aerial photographs	صور جوية
census data	بيانات إحصاء السكان
computerized data	بيانات مُحوسَبة
whether or not	سواء أكان ... أم لم يكن
satellite photography	تصوير الأقمار الصناعية
cultural context	سياق ثقافي
let alone	ناهيك عن
teaching aids	وسائل تعليمية
channels of information	قنوات المعلومات
to such an extent that	إلى حدّ أنَّ
value judgments	أحكام قِيميَّة
congnitive perspective	منظور معرفي
the world over	في جميع أنحاء العالم
adult life	حياة البلوغ
rural and urban landscapes	مناظر ريفية ومدينية
school journeys	رحلات مدرسية
acquisition of knowledge	اكتساب المعرفة
mass media	وسائل الإعلام
direct contact	اتصال مباشر
direct experience	خبرة مباشر

Exercise 1 . *Translate the previous passage into Arabic.*

Exercise 2. *Fill in this table with the suitable English derivatives whenever possible, and write down the Arabic equivalents of all the words.*

Verb		Noun		Adjective	
English	**Arabic**	**English**	**Arabic**	**English**	**Arabic**
		map			
		photograph			
		television			
				limited	
				visual	
		mediation			
				remote	
live					
		colour			
distort					
				familiar	
judge					
		event			
				separated	
perceive					
				evident	
		migrant			
experience					
				integral	

Exercise 3. *Translate these expressions :*

little by little	——————	year by year	——————
day by day	——————	hour by hour	——————
step by step	——————	dollar by dollar	——————
one by one	——————	city by city	——————

UNIT 8

THE USE OF THIS
COMPASS

WE have seen how it is possible to find direction by means of landmarks the sun. and the stars. But it may easily happen on a foggy day or a cloudy night that none of these can be seen. How does the traveler on land, or the sailor on the sea, find his way then ?   He uses an instrument called a compass.

Long ago the Chinese found that a little bar of magnetic iron always pointed in the same direction if it were allowed to swing freely. Even a bar of ordinary iron ⎯ say, a small poker ⎯will always come to rest pointing in the same direction   if suspended by a string about its middle. But if the bar is also **magnetized**, it will come to rest much more quickly.

At first the little " bar " or needle was floated on water, but men found it more useful to suspend it on fine pivot, so that it could swing freely and easily. The Arab borrowed the idea from the Chinese, and it was the Arabs who passed on the knowledge to Europeans.

The compass needle, then, points always in the some direction. Why, it is difficult to explain perhaps when you know more science, and learn more about the laws obeyed by magnets, you will begin to understand why a magnetic needle always points to the same spot on the earth's surface.

Simple exercises may now be devised to prove that a magnetised needle always comes to rest pointing in the same direction. Any number of needles may be sufficiently magnetised by rubbing them on a large bar or horseshoe magnet. Children may than experiment with their needles both at school and at home. They will discover the ad-vantage of the pivoted over the floated needle, and the value of marking the north-pointing end. It is now easy to understand the value of the compass card which rides on the black of the needle, and is carried by it in its swing.

The teacher, of course. Has for school use a large mariner's compass. Which readily takes to pieces to show the parts. He shows the needle (from which the card has been removed) and the pivot on which it swing. He allows it to come to rest side by side with a magnetised needle floating in a basin of water. Both point in the same direction He next fixes a blank circular card on the needle's back, and shows the advantage of it by marking on it the cardinal points, which children will readily give him.

CONSTRUCTION OF SIMPLE COMPASS CARDS

On a card let children draw a large circle, and through its centre two diameters at right angles to each other. Name the points N., S., E,. W. A few exercises will show that these four alone are very inadequate. Insert N.E., NW., S.W., by drawing thinner diameters midway between each pair of those already drown. After further

Helpful Vocabulary :

use of the compass	استخدام البوصلة
traveler on land	المسافر في البر
sailor on the sea	البحّار في البحر
magnetic iron	حديد مغناطيسي
will come to rest	سَيِسْتقِرّ
if suspended	إذا عُلِّق
compass needle	إبرة البوصلة
magnetic needle	إبرة مُمغْنَطة
horseshoe magnet	مغناطيس على شكل حذاء الفرس
experiment with	يُجَرّب
floated needle	الإبرة المُعَوَّمة
north-pointing end	الطرف المشير إلى الشَّمال
for school use	للاستخدام المدرسي
mariner's compass	بوصلة البحّار ، بوصلة بحرية
take to pieces	تنقسم إلى أجزاء
basin of water	حوض ماء

Exercise 1 . *Translate the previous passage into Arabic.*

Exercise 2. *Fill in this table with the suitable English derivatives whenever possible, and write down the Arabic equivalents of all the words.*

Verb		Noun		Adjective	
English	Arabic	English	Arabic	English	Arabic
		sun			
		direction			
				possible	
		star			
				foggy	
sail					
		cloud			
travel					
use					
		magnet			
swing					
		Arab			
suspend					
		law			
				easy	
allow					
pass					
		exercise			

Exercise 3. *What are the two translations of each verb, as a verb and as a noun ?*

rest	_____	_____	point	_____	_____
sun	_____	_____	surface	_____	_____
land	_____	_____	number	_____	_____
iron	_____	_____	show	_____	_____

UNIT 9

The PERIOD OF THE WEARRING STATES

I N S T E A D   of progressing towards the ideals of a Great Com- monwealth as conceived by the k 'ung school, the Chinese kingdom further degenerated in the days of Tseng Ts'an and Tzu-ssu. The Chou sovereign remained on the throne, but his authority was disregarded and his prerogative as the son of Heaven was confined to religious matters alone. In conse- quence, even his norminal kingship was challenged by the feudal lords of the great states. In the course of time these rulers assumed one after another the presumptuous title of king, thus making themselves equals of the Chou sovereign not only in fact but also in name. what a severe blow it would have been to master k'ung, the feudal torch-bearer had he lived on to these unruly times !

The period after Master k'ung is known in history as that of the Warring states. An appropriate name, it speaks elo-quently of the turbulent conditions of the age. As a result of the continuous wars the political situation in China was greatly changed, and seven big states now emerged to over-run practically the whole country. These were Ch'I in the east, Ch'u in the south, Ch'in in the north-west, yon, a new power, in the north-east, and Hen, wei, and Chao, off-spring of the mighty Tsin, in the north. At the same time, those small principalities that had flourished in Master k'ung's time had been either eliminated from the scene or squeezed between their strong neighbours with barely any space for a lingering existence. The entire history of the period was therefore on of endless struggle for supremacy among the great powers.

In an ago where might was right, the rulers of these con- tending states all strove to build up a powerful army for the

Pursuit of their selfish ends. Their desire for conquest was insatiable; their ambitions were overwhelming. Wars, moreover, were no longer governed by a feudal code of honour as in the olden days, but fought to a finish in the most devastating manner possible with a great deal of blood-shed. Lands were annexed and subjects enslaved. while enemy soldiers were massacred by the thousands. On the debris of fallen cities and the mounds of the dead there rose to eminence and power intriguing politicians. Ruthless gene-rals, and autocratic rulers, who all wallowed in wealth at the expense of the common people.

With increasing riches and power the kings of the War-ring states indulged themselves to such an extent that their lusts and dissipations belittled even the licentious excesses of the earlier days. In almost every state the rulers lived in great pomp. They wore gorgeous garments ornamented with pearls and jade; owned carved boats and embroidered carriages; lived in magnificent places with porches and pavilions. They also indulged in feasting and carousing. The lord of a large state was served with a hundred courses, so much so that 'eyes could not see all the dishes, hands could not handle them all, and the mouth could not taste them all.' Even the minister of a small principality like Wey, ac- cording to a contemporary witness, had in his house hun-dreds of decorated vehicles, hundreds of horses fed with grain, and several hundred concubines clothed in finery. From these stories the extravagance of a great king can be well imagined.

The above picture affords a striking contrast to the sad plight of the peasants, who were weighed down by the trip burdens of war, taxation. And conscription. Their miseries were graphically described by Meng K'o, who, speaking of his time, asserted that while there was fat meat in the lord's kitchen and three were fat horses in the lord's stable the people were a picture of hunger and privation. Meng K'o further stated that in times of plenty immense stores of provisions were consumed by armies ingaged in war, while in calamitous years the old and feeble died by the thousands in valleys and ditches, and the able-bodied were scattered about to the four quarters of the globe. Such disorganization of the rural community constituted a serious threat to the very fabric of feudal society

Helpful Vocabulary :

warring states	دول متحاربة
Chinese kingdom	المملكة الصينية
Was confined to	كان مقتصراً على
nominal kingship	مَلكية اسمية
in the course of time	مع مرور الوقت
severe blow	ضربة قاسية
had he lived	لو أنه عاش
turbulent conditions	ظروف مضطربة
political situation	الوضع السياسي
struggle for supremacy	صراع على السيادة
might was right	كان الحق للقوة
selfish ends	أهداف أنانية
desire for conquest	الرغبة في الفتوحات
in the most devastating manner possible	بأكبر تدمير ممكن
... subjects enslaved ...	مواطنون اسْتُعبدوا
Debris of fallen cities	أنقاض المدن المهزومة
Increasing riches	ثروات متزايدة
Great pomp	أُبَّهَة عظيمة
magnificent palaces	قصور رائعة
so much so that	إلى حدّ أنَّ
contemporary witness	شاهد معاصر
trip burdens	أعباء ثالوث

Exercise 1 . *Translate the previous passage into Arabic.*

Exercise 2. *Fill in this table with the suitable English derivatives whenever possible, and write down the Arabic equivalents of all the words.*

Verb		Noun		Adjective	
English	**Arabic**	**English**	**Arabic**	**English**	**Arabic**
degenerate					
disregard					
				nominal	
assume					
				feudal	
		might			
				eloquent	
flourish					
		power			
strive					
		conquest			
				dead	
		ambition			
				magnificent	
decorate					
		witness			
				extravagant	
belittle					

Exercise 3. *These words can be used as verbs and nouns Translate them, showing the two usages .*

name   _____   _____   neighbor   _____   _____

age   _____   _____   struggle   _____   _____

spring   _____   _____   end   _____   _____

war   _____   _____   finish   _____   _____

UNIT 10

THE HUMANITY
OF ASIA

The need today is for philosophers and schools_whether in
Asia or Europe or Africa or the Americas_who will address
Themselves to the human situation. The need now is to talk not
About geographic destiny but about human destiny.

— *NORMAN COSINS*

Asia is people. People till Asia's earth, write Asia's poetry, make Asia's laws, fight Asia's ware, and dream Asia's dreams. Asians are people with a destiny. Few Westerners grasp the meaning of this destiny, because few outside Asia fully comprehend the humanity of Asian. They think of them first as inhabitants of a region called Asia, and only second as fellow human beings.

The humanity which Asians share with the rest of mankind and which nourishes the seeds of Asian destiny is overlooked by most foreigners in their preoccupation with the cultural differences which distinguish Asians from themselves. This preoccupation with eye-catching differences blinds them to the basic human needs, human drives, and human aspirations of the Asian people. They do not see the dynamic human forces which move Asian to act. They see only the acts, and these are acts Westerner would not normally perform. The Asian mother who sells her daughter, the Asian laborer who smokes his pipe of opium, the two Japanese lovers who commit suicide together, the Indian who wanders off to become an ascetic leaving his family behind_these are some of the acts often head-lined in Western minds as the peculiar substance of Asian humanity

Most people cannot imagine the anguish of this Asian mother pushed to a decision by the spectre of famine. They do not under-stand the harshness of the laborer,s life relieved only by a better world given him by the opium pipe. Many cannot appreciate the despair that grips those Japanese lovers when they find every avenue of a future happiness together closed to them. Few people in the

World outside of India comprehend the spirit that moves an Indian   ascetic to live a life of constant sacrifice. Thus, most Westerners   are led to think of Asians in terms of the mysterious and the in-   scrutable. People who act so differently seem alien, even frighten-ing.

It becomes easy to reduce Asians to stereotypes. Indians are ascetic to live a life of constant sacrifice. Thus, most westerners   are led to think of Asians in terms of the mysterious and the in-scrutable. People who act so differently seem alien, even frighten-ing.

It becomes easy to reduce Asians to stereotypes. Indians are "mystical," "cow-worshippers," and, until recently, "a peaceful peo-ple." Japan is a land where is a land where all men have buck teeth and all women wear beautiful kimonos. It is also the land of the cherry blossom festivals, people with soldiers who always fight fanatically and make suicide charges. Tow prominent writers about Asian people have commented with insight upon these stereotypes with regard to Japan. Frank Gibney in *five Gentlemen of Japan* writes:"it is hard to pour them] the five Japanese individuals he is describing [into the rigid casts of ' Japanese character' which foreigners at different times have constructed… it is hard to fit them into the land of Madame Butterfly and never-ending cherry blossom festivals, faith-fully and gullibly described by generations of Western tourists." James A. Michener in the floating World states: "about the only generalization I could accept about the Japanese is that they will all have black hair."

Thinking in terms of stereotypes has influenced Americans _and others_ to draw a line separating 'Eastern' man from" Western" man. On one side of the line there is an "Eastern" way of life_ alien, quaint, and mysterious. On the other side of the line there is a "Western" way of life _ human, normal, and understandable. This belief is classically expressed in Kipling, statement: "East is East, and West is West. And never the twain shall meet."

Kipling, like many today, was unfamiliar with the process known as cultural diffusion. Both "Both "Easterners" have bor-rowed material products, as ideas, mores, and other intangi-bles, from each other and adapted them to their own cultures. Many non-Asians have learned to taste and like the many spices that come from Asia, enjoy the coolness of silk pajamas upon the skin, and delight in the green depths of their jade rings. Pajamas are a cultural import from India, while silk and jade rings originated in china and southeast Asia.

Helpful Vocabulary :

till Asia's earth	يحرثون أرض آسيا
grasp the meaning	يفهم المعنى
humanity of Asians	إنسانية الآسيويين
rest of mankind	باقي البشَر
cultural differences	فروق ثقافية
blind them to	تُعْميهم عن
human drives	الدوافع الإنسانية
human aspirations	الطموحات الإنسانية
harshness of life	قسوة الحياة
Indian ascetic	زاهد هندي
suicide charges	هَجْمات انتحارية
Japanese character	الشخصية اليابانية
Eastern man	الرجل الشرقي
cultural diffusion	انتشار ثقافي
cultural import	مُسْتوردَ ثقافي
human needs	حاجات إنسانية
East is East	الشرق هو الشرق
West is west	الغرب هو الغرب

Exercise 1 . *Translate the previous passage into Arabic.*

Exercise 2. *Fill in this table with the suitable English derivatives whenever possible, and write down the Arabic equivalents of all the words.*

Verb		Noun		Adjective	
English	**Arabic**	**English**	**Arabic**	**English**	**Arabic**
write					
		war			
dream					
		destiny			
nourish					
		Asia			
differ					
		region			
				peculiar	
aspire					
		suicide			
sell					
				recent	
		despair			
				mysterious	

Exercise 3. *How do you translate these pairs ?*

Austria	————————	Australia `	————————
Venus	————————	Venice	————————
the west	————————	the West	————————
the east	————————	the East	————————
carton	————————	cartoon	————————
stationery	————————	stationary	————————
effect	———————affect		————————
fact	————————	fiction	————————

UNIT 11

LITERATURE AS A SPECIALIST SUBJECT

The main difference between the use of representational materials as part or language learning. and the use of literature as a specialist discipline for L2 students, is one of *focus*. Where in language learning the emphasis has been on theme or subject matter for the specific aim of language development, in literature study the emphasis will be on text , author and period. There is no need for the communicative and interactive principles, already found, suddenly to be discarded as we move into the realm of specialisation. English for Academic purposes need present no more difficulties, or arcane mysteries, than any other kind of English study.

The methodology so far discussed in this book is wholly applicable to the context of academic English study_say for a degree in English, or for a teacher-training qualification. The approaches we have seen are indeed an indispensable introduction to the study of literature. Too often in university all over the world, literature study is not related to language learning; one is considered something of a superior discipline, the other an inferior exercise (often entrusted to lower-level personnel). Language learning and literary study are interdependent and in a specialist context, should be seen as complementary at all stages in the educational process.

Only in this way can the situation be avoided whereby an L2 learner at beginner or false-beginner level finds that Chaucer is the first author on the programme. The absurdity of learning the different usages of the simple present and present Continuous tenses while battling through the 'Nun's priest's Tale' may seem far-fetched, but is, in fact, a not uncommon occurrence in English L2 degree courses.

The emphasis on the historical study of literature in an academic contexi is not threatened by a contrastive approach to selected passages from major and minor writers. The approach is a necessary introduction not only to a wide range of writers, styles and content, but also to ways of looking at text and of examining them in depth.

Where the exploitation of a text for non-specialist learners may stop short of close examination of, say, metonymy and metaphor, stylistic devices or the historical context of the writing, the teacher of a more specialized class can move on with the same texts to investigate those elements that will bring the students into contact with such features of historical language, authorial style and period context that are required in history of literature curriculum at tertiary level.

The emphasis on the test as the starting-point for all literature study is of paramount importance. The metalanguage of literary study which can comfortably be avoided in non-specialist use of representational materials, has here to be integrated into the apparatus. Basically, the teachniques applied in terms of text selection and grading, apparatus, and classroom practice will remain the same: the variable is the teaching aim. whether the level is secondary school or university does not actually make a great difference in the initial stages; beginners are beginners whether they are fourteen, twenty, or sixty years old. There is, of course, the question of students being mature enough to handle the themes presented, but, to all intents and purposes, if a group of texts is going to work at all with L2 students. the maturity level and the intellectual level tie closely with the basic question of accessibility and the importance of what the readers are required to do with the text .

A literature study curriculum has to make greater demands on students. Quite simply, the learning objectives include literary aspects as well as the language-learning aspects which interest the non-specialist teacher and learner. So, in addition to the deeper study of individual texts, there will necessarily be more texts from aider range of periods and contexts in a specialized programme. The structure of such a programme will move more rapidly to extended reading: from extract to short story to novel, for example; or from a scene to a complete play; or from one poem to reading of several. The thematic content of one text is thus seen in comparison with an extended thematic and stylistic range. Back-ground, historical context and literary developments, however, are always best related to the text the students start from. To return to an example quoted in Chapter 6, specialist students who have read complementary passages from Animal Farm and paradise Lost can refer their reading to the historical, social and political context in which these two very different works (which, we have seen, share the theme of rebellion) were written.

I deliberately underline this example in order to show now precon-ceived notions about author, period or text can come between the student and an interactive reading of the text. Million, thought of as the creator of an epic poem on the Fall of Man-which was intended to explain Man's 'disobedience' and his place in the great scheme of things-is a considerably more daunting Milton than the one students can alternatively be introduced to, who wrote about the violent rebellion of some independent angels in Heaven. Similarly, the Orwell who is seen writing a sharp allegory against totalitarianism is quite different from the author of a passage where animals take over a farm from humans. The tale, not the teller, must come first-or, as Brecht put it to his actors, 'show me, don'ts tell me. The text is the showing, all the rest is input which comes between the reader and the text. Of course, it is highly relevant and, indeed, useful input. But when information about the text is give before the reader has the chance to experience the text for him-or herself, it gets in the way, it impedes direct interaction, conditions the reader's reactions and responses, destroys the innocence of reading.

Helpful Vocabulary :

L2 students	طلاب اللغة الثانية
language development	النموّ اللغوي
literature study	دراسة الأدب
realm of specialization	مجال التخصص
English for Academic Purposes	الإنجليزية لأهداف أكاديمية ، الإنجليزية لأهدف دراسية
Indispensable introduction	مقدمة لا غنى عنها
contrastive approach	نهج تقابلي ، نهجٌ مقارَن
examine in depth	يتفحص بعمق
non-specialist learners	متعلمون غير مختصين
authorial style	أسلوب المؤلِّف
period context	سياق الحِقْبة
literature curriculum	منهج الأدب
of paramount importance	ذو أهمية فائقة
text selection	اختيار النصوص
specialized program	برنامج متخصص
extended reading	قراءة موسَّعة
complementary passages	قِطَعٌ تكميلية
preconceived notions	أفكار مُسْبَقة
come between	تَحُولُ بين
epic poem	قصيدة ملحمية
violent rebellion	تمرد عنيف
direct interaction	تفاعل مباشر

Exercise 1 . *Translate the previous passage into Arabic.*

Exercise 2. *Fill in this table with the suitable English derivatives whenever possible, and write down   the Arabic equivalents of all the words.*

Verb		Noun		Adjective	
English	**Arabic**	**English**	**Arabic**	**English**	**Arabic**
represent					
		literature			
interact					
		emphasis			
		mystery			
				applicable	
				superior	
		context			
occur					
				superior	
		battle			
require					
				minor	
extend					
		question			
				human	
begin					
		author			
				sharp	

Exercise 3. *Translate these pairs :*

examiner ——————— examinee ———————

trainer ——————— trainee ———————

payer ——————— payee ———————

employer ——————— employee ———————

UNIT 12

THE PURPOSES AND
FUNCTION OF
THE STATE

For what purposes does the state exist. This question has been asked many times in every ago from the beginning of political society. It is indeed the fundamental question of politics. Should the state do a certain thing, or refrain from doing it ? Different answers have been given by patricians and plebeians, cavaliers and puritans, and individualists and socialists as each group has urged that the adoption of its own ideas would best subserve the interests of society as a whole. The building of irrigation works in ancient Mesopotamia, the protection of commerce in Carthage , the development of the cultured man in Athens__ all must have appeared to be essential lunctions of the state along with protection from invasion and maintenance of order. In more recent times, state action for the enhancement of resources for the proper distribution of wealth, and for social services have seemed important. There is no single best theory concern-ing the purposes of the state that will be valid at all times and for all societies. The political scientist should consider how far advanced in civilization a society is, the stage of its political development, the nature of the problems that it faces, and its needs and aspiration. Changes in social conditions beget altered concepts of the purposes of the state.

THE PURPOSES OF THE STATE

A brief analysis of purposes provides a useful frame of refer-ence for evaluating theories of state functions. The purposes or ends of the state are the ultimate aims for which it exists.

Establishment of Order. A primary end of the state is to in-sure freedom from invasion and to secure domestic tranquility and justice for its people. The existence of the state can hardly be justified unless it succeeds reasonably will in achieving this end. The attainment of all other objectives depends on the suc- cess of the state in securing the highest degree of order consistent with the liberties of individuals and of groups in the society.

Promotion of Individual Welfare. Nearly all modern theory stresses the importance of the individual. The very existence of the state creates a condition in which individual progress can be realized. Whether the individual fares best through decisions "made for him" or through decisions "or through decisions" mad by him "constitutes an essential difference between totalitarian and democratic theory. Democratic theory recognizes the inherent worth of the individual and seeks to provide the most favorable conditions, consistent with the interests of society as a whole, under which he may complete the fulfillment of his personality. Among these conditions are the protection of personal rights and effective participation in government.

Promotion of General Welfare. A third end of the state is the development of public capacities. This involves care for the common interests of the society and provision for united ac- tion in achieving goals which individuats or associations can not achieve by themselves. It involves the reconciliation of interests among groups and between individuals or groups and the society as a whole.

Promotion of Morality. One of the oldest and must persistent theories declares that an essential purpose of the state is to pro- mote morality among its people. Applications of the theory in various ages have usually been attempts to impose upon a citi- zenry one standard of morality, one code of conduct, or one religion. There is something incongruous in the use of force with resulting loss in the maintenance of order (moral action depends upon voluntary behavior). However. The state is not oliged to remain neutral on such maters. It may punish vicious and criminal conduct by criminal laws and it may en-courage good conduct by means of various reward.

THE FUNCTIONS OF THE STATES

Theorists may be in substantial agreement concerning the pur-poses of the state and yet be poles apart in their ideas of state function. The *functions* of the state may be defined in terms of the particular activities in which it engages.

Helpful Vocabulary :

political society	مجتمع سياسي
protection of commerce	حماية التجارة
cultured man	الإنسان المثقف
maintenance of order	حفظ النظام
enhancement of resources	تنمية الموارد
distribution of wealth	توزيع الثروة
single best theory	النظرية المُثلى الوحيدة
altered concepts	مفاهيم متغيرة
frame of reference	إطارُ مرجعيةٍ
evaluating theories	نظريات التقييم
state functions	وظائف الدولة
ultimate aims	أهداف نهائية
individual welfare	رفاهة الفرد
the very existence of the state	وجود الدولة ذاته
personal rights	حقوق شخصية
effective participation	مشاركة فعّالة
general welfare	الخير العام ، الرفاهة العامة
reconciliation of interests	التوفيق بين المصالح
criminal conduct	سلوك إجرامي
applications of the theory	تطبيقات النظرية
attempts to impose	محاولات لفرض
resulting loss	خسارة ناجمة

Exercise 1 . *Translate the previous passage into Arabic.*

Exercise 2. *Fill in this table with the suitable English derivatives whenever possible, and write down   the Arabic equivalents of all the words.*

Verb		Noun		Adjective	
English	**Arabic**	**English**	**Arabic**	**English**	**Arabic**
exist					
Protect					
		function			
				social	
beget					
		politics			
evaluate					
				free	
		end			
invade					
do					
		aspiration			
				individual	
		wealth			
				favorable	
alter					
consider					
		progress			

Exercise 3. *Translate these words , showing two different meanings :*

purpose	——————	——————	answer	——————	—————
question	——————	——————	interest	——————	—————
function	——————	——————	change	——————	—————
single	——————	——————	stage	——————	—————
aim	——————	——————	state	——————	—————

UNIT 13

CHANING STUDENT NEEDS AND A TEACHER'S ROLE

There is little doubt that educators face more intense challenges with students today than they did 30 years ago. Students come to school socially and emotionally depleted and ill-prepared to learn. At home, students live with parental indifference, social isolation hopelessness, and even physical and emotional abuse and neglect Some students deal with even more difficult home situations such as parental mental illness, alcoholism, drug addiction, or criminal be- havior. All these unfavorable social conditions place young people at risk of becoming involved in unproductive or even self-destructive behavior. An at-risk or high-risk youth is defined as one who is facing two obstacles to healthy development: the inner obstacle of unmet needs and the outer obstacle of increasing environmental stresses (Burns, 1994). Even young people who come from loving, supportive homes can become at risk, especially during adolescence, because of negative peer pressure or antagonistic environmental conditions. Adverse living conditions are threatening the healthy emotional and social development of children. They are obstacles that young people must successfully overcome if they are to grow up to be productive well-adjusted adults. Unfortunately, many young people simply survive these adverse situations by engaging in their own self-destructive activities, such as drug and alcohol abuse, dropping out of school, or gang activities. Such self-destructive behaviors place these kids at risk for perpetuating the cycle of poverty, abuse, or criminal activity with which they grew up. The door to what other-wise may have been bright futures close.

As educators, we are all too familiar with the adverse situations students deal with daily and with the feelings of hopelessness and powerlessness as we watch young people set themselves on a path-

64

way to self-destruction. We know the problems. Frustrated,disheat-ened, and sometimes overwhelmed. we want answers. We need to learn effective, appropriate ways to deal with the complicated hu-man situations we must face daily in the classroom.

This book describes appropriate effective ways for teachers to help students deal with the adverse situations they face. It illustrates ways teachers can make a difference for the growing number of students living in high-risk situations or living at-risk lives. Based on a qualitative study completed in 1994 (Deiro, 1994), this book illus- trates an appropriate role teachers can assume to help these students. This role is not another add-on to further overload a teacher's current busy schedule. The suggested role involves teacher behaviors that are natural, intrinsic parts of a teacher's responsibilities. In essence, this book suggest ways for teachers to simultaneously improve their teaching skills and help at-risk students.

The book begins with a discussion about ways teachers can make a difference for students by presenting evidence that demonstrates the importance of building meaningful connections with young peo-ple. It affirms that the most powerful and effective way teachers can help young people overcome the negative impact of adverse situ-ation and become productive citizens is by developing a close and trusting relationship with their students. The book first establishes that the healthy development of children in today,s society is de-pendent on more adults becoming meaningfully involved in chil-dren's lives. Then using this premise, it explores an appropriate role teachers can assume that allows them to become meaningfully in-volved in the lives of their students.

Bonding as a key to
Healthy Adolescent Development

Bounding with prosocial adults has been identified as the key protective factor buffering children against the influence of adverse situations (Benard,1991;Brook, Brook, Gordon, Whiteman,&Cohen, 1990; Hawkins,Catalano, & Miller,1992). Prosocial here refers to individuals who obey the laws of society and respect our social norms. For example, bonds with a parent who smokes marijuana or who disrespects the law do not foster healthy social and emotional development, whereas bonds with a parent who models good work habits, chooses not to abuse drugs, and shows active concern for the welfare of others do promote healthy development.

Helpful Vocabulary :

intense challenges	تحديات شديدة
parental indifference	لا مبالاة الوالدين
social isolation	عُزْلة اجتماعية
home situations	أوضاع منزلية ، ظروف منزلية
mental illness	مرض نفسي
drug addiction	إدمان المخدرات
self-destructive behavior	سلوك مدمر للذات
healthy development	نموّ سليم ، نموّ صحّيّ
unmet needs	حاجات غير مُشْبَعَة
increasing environmental stresses	ضغوطات بيئية متزايدة
negative peer pressure	ضغط الأقران السلبي
well-adjusted adults	بالغون حسنو التكيف
gang activities	نشاطات العصابات
cycle of poverty	دائرة الفقر
hopelessness and powerlessness	اليأس والعجز
appropriate role	الدور المناسب
disrespect the law	لا يحترم القانون
prosocial adult	بالغ متوائم اجتماعياً
trusting relationship	علاقة ثقة
busy schedule	جدول مزدحم
overload the teacher	يُثْقِل المعلّم

Exercise 1 . *Translate the previous passage into Arabic.*

Exercise 2. *Fill in this table with the suitable English derivatives whenever possible, and write down   the Arabic equivalents of all the words.*

Verb		Noun		Adjective	
English	**Arabic**	**English**	**Arabic**	**English**	**Arabic**
		face			
				intense	
		behavior			
		emotion			
				powerless	
base					
				hopeless	
illustrate					
		answer			
				frustrated	
		factor			
				indifferent	
		health			
explore					
improve					
		situation			
involve					
		concern			

Exercise 3. *Translate these pairs :*

student	طالب	pupil	تلميذ
little	_____	few	_____
some	_____	several	_____
much	_____	many	_____
child	_____	infant	_____
adolescent	_____	adult	_____

UNIT 14

TEACHING METHOD COMPARED WITH OTHER EDUCATIONAL CONCEPTS

As we have already said. it would be irrational to examine one educational phenomenon in isolation from another: when examining a concept it is incumbent upon the examiner to determine its proper position and its principal associations with other concepts. The deceptively simple daily scholastic routine is a process at once so complex and dynamic as to rule out an examination of the concept of teaching methods in isolation lest the reality should be distorted. In view of this. we purport to inscribe' the concept of teaching methods into the 'circumference' of education as such and bind it closely to the current problems of Soviet education theory and daily school practice

It may be appropriate to in invoke an analogy between the linkages between educa-tional categories applied to teaching and that of the components used in building construction.

The builders first come out with an idea or a design for the future edifice. as do the educationists in relation to the educational goal. The principles of building each-nology and architecture govern the realization of a design in much the same way as the theoretical principles of teaching govern the realization of teaching goals. The building materials specified in the architectural plans evoke analogy with the sub-stance or content of education. The methods and teachniques of construction, pre-supposing the use of specific technical and other equipment, may be compared with the methods and techniques of teaching. The detailed organization of the works, designers and engineers on the site is another essential component of construction similar to the organization of the educational process. The above analogies serve to emphasize the integrity of the main components introduced into the process of education similar to the integrity of the main components introduced into the process of education similar to the integrity of building components introduced into the process of construction. However. The provision of all the components making up a modern human being is a much more challenging enterprise than the creation of an edifice, no matter how grandiose.

Goals and methods

Teaching methods are first and foremost connected with teaching goals, either directly or indirectly, through the content of education. In a modern socialist society (1) :

The purpose of public education in the USSR is to train highly educated. Comprehensively developed and active builders of communist society, reared on the ideas of Marxism-Lenin- ism, in the spirit of respect for Soviet laws and socialist law and order, communist attitude to work, physically healthy and capable of successfully working in different areas of economic, social and cultural construction, actively participating in social and state activities, ready to selflessly defend their socialist Homeland, to preserve and augment her material and culture wealth, protect and preserve nature. Public education in the USSR is called upon to ensure the development and the satisfaction of the cultural and intellectual requirements of Soviet man.

Proceeding from the Marxist-Leninist propositions with regard to the all- round and harmonious development of the personality, one can describe the goals of educa- tion as ideological and political, moral and ethical, intellectual, aesthetic and phy- sical; the interconnections are sufficient for them to be viewed as a whole. Personal qualities may in turn be described as living in the areas of competence, skills. Convictions. behaviours, attitudes and action patterns. One of the principal object-tives of education is to inculcate communist ideology and moral principles, which presupposes a scientific understanding of nature. an understanding closely linked with daily life. Attitudes to work are also considered vitai- an honest attitude to work; an ardent desire to work for the common good; not merely for personal profit but as long as work is identified with public benefits-such are the qualities highly cherished by the communists. It is at work and through study that one develops a sense of being part of a community-an organized entity- a sense of discipline and duty. Basically, it amounts to the formation of such universally cherished human qualities as mutual respect, mutual aid, loyalty, sincerity, self-criticism and mod-esty.

It is by motivating every school boy and girl to participate in collective socially-useful work, in working out socialist standards of mutual attitudes and behaviours that one should be able to mould a personality worthy of a new socialist society. Marx emphasized the importance of encouraging the individual to interact actively and creatively with his social environment, as well as of motivating children to participate (as far as educational goats are concerned) in the work of adults. The process of making a man involves the assimilation and careful processing of human cultural heritage, since it is man who creates the world and his own self. Combining productive work with study is understood by Marxists as the only means of moulding a harmoniously developed personality']2[. Also of importance to all- round personality development are proper education. good health, and honest morals and ethics. Thus, education takes its bearings from a profoundly humanistic approach. Viewed from this humanistic stance, the goals of formal education pre- suppose an active cognitive effort on the part of the pupils so that they have a scientific method of acquiring knowledge which can be used to acquire more knowledge in the future.

It is already at the school desk that a foundation is laid for continuous learning, involving the development from an early age of a lifelong quest for knowledge, which may assume the many and varied forms of self-instruction and. as a rule, go hand-in-hand with social and productive activities; or else, continuous learning may be combined with formal education in colleges and universities. The soviet Communist Party programme states: … the education of the younger generation should be closely linked with daily life and productive work. While the adults could combine work in the sphere of production with continuous study, which can only be of benefit to society]3[.

Helpful Vocabulary :

educational phenomenon	ظاهرة تربوية
principal associations	علاقات رئيسية
teaching methods	أساليب التدريس
daily scholastic routine	الرَّتَابَة المدرسية اليومية
in view of this	في هذا الإطار
current problems	المشكلات الحالية
building construction	إقامة بناية
theoretical principles	مبادئ نظرية
realization of teaching goals	تحقيق الأهداف التعليمية
educational process	العملية التربوية
above analogies	القياسات المذكورة أعلاه
integrity of components	تكامل المكونات
intellectual requirements	متطلبات ذهنية
action patterns	أنماط التصرّف
moral principles	مبادئ أخلاقية
closely linked with	مرتبط بشدة بـــ
the common good	الصالح العام
sense of discipline	إحساس بالانضباط
mutual respect	احترام متبادل
social environment	بيئة اجتماعية
cultural heritage	التراث الثقافي
all-round personality development	نمو الشخصية المتكاملة
lifelong quest for knowledge	طلب المعرفة مدى الحياة ، السعي الدائم وراء المعرفة

Exercise 1 . *Translate the previous passage into Arabic.*

Exercise 2. *Fill in this table with the suitable English derivatives whenever possible, and write down the Arabic equivalents of all the words.*

Verb		Noun		Adjective	
English	**Arabic**	**English**	**Arabic**	**English**	**Arabic**
distort					
				complex	
examine					
introduce					
		provision			
challenge					
		construction			
				productive	
emphasize					
		equipment			
				continuous	
motivate					
		education			
				profound	
acquire					
		foundation			
				sufficient	
presuppose					

Exercise 3. *Translate these words related to the same field of education :*

school	_____	college	_____
university	_____	institute	_____
institution	_____	kindergarten	_____
nursery	_____	high school	_____

UNIT 15

SOCIAL AND MORAL   DEVELOPMENT

At the end of this chapter you should be able to:

1   describe and evaluate psychodynamic, learning theory and cognitive approaches to development;

2   compare and contrast these three developmental approaches;

3   describe psychodynamic. Social learning theory and cognitive approaches to moral development;

4   evaluate these approaches in the light of empirical evidence;

5   briefly describe some research into

    (a)   the effects of parental discipline and

    (b)   peer-group influences on moral development.

INTRODUCTION

Three major theoretical approaches have contributed to out knowledge of social and moral behaviour:

1   the psychodynamic approach which arises from Freud's theory of personality   development;

2   the learning theory approach, which is based on the work of the early Behaviourists such as Watson, Pavlov and Thorndike, and currently upheld by psychologists such as Skinner and Bandura;

3   the cognitive approach which is derived largely from Piaget's theory of cognitive development.

Each approach will be considered in turn.

SECTION I: PSYCHODYNAMIC APPROACH

INTRODUCTION

Freud's psychoanalytic view of child development has had a   profound effect on psychological thinking since its introduction in the early part of this century.

Originally trained as a doctor, Freud's interest in neurology led him to specialize in nervous disorders. He noted that many neurotic disorders exhibited by his patients appeared to stem from former traumatic experiences rather than from physical complaints. Freud gradually developed his now famous psychoanalytic treatment of emotional and personality disorders.

Psychoanalysis involves the use of three major techniques:

1. 'free association' — encouraging patients to express the free flow of thoughts entering their minds;
2. analysis of dreams;
3. interpretation of 'slips of speech' and other 'accidental events'.

Each of these techniques, Freud believed, would penetrate the **unconscious mind** of the patient and reveal thoughts, feelings and motivations of which the patient was not consciously aware.

From this early work emerged Freud's monumental theory of the human mind and personality. Central to the theory are his belief in:

- the importance of early childhood experiences for later personality and emotional development:
- the existence of the unconscious mind harbouring repressed   memories which motivate and influence conscious thoughts and behaviour;
- the existence of **instinctual drives** which motivate and regulate human behaviour even in childhood. The source of these drives is psychic energy, and the most important, the **libido**, is sexual in nature. Libido is a force which compels humans to behave in ways which are likely to reproduce the species.
- the importance of **defence mechanisms** such as **repression**   (removing painful experiences from conscious memory); **regression**   (reverting back to earlier ways of behaving in order to escape form stressful events); **projection** (expressing one's own disturbing feeling or attitudes as though they arose from another person); **sublimation** (expressing basic drives, for example aggressive tendencies, in a substitute activity— such as art).

An important concept introduced by Freud is that of **identification**, a psychological mechanism which aims to explain the increasing similarity between the behaviour of children an older generations.

Helpful Vocabulary :

learning theory	نظرية التعلُّم
cognitive approaches	المناهج المعرفية
moral development	نمو أخلاقي
empirical evidence	دليل تجريبي ، دليل حِسِّيَ
parental discipline	تأديب الوالدين
peer-group influences	تأثير جماعة الأقران
moral behaviour	السلوك الأخلاقي
personality development	نموّ الشخصية
psychoanalytic view	النظرة النفسية التحليلية
nervous disorders	اضطرابات عصبية
personality disorders	اضطرابات الشخصية
neurotic disorders	اضطرابات عُصَابية
free association	الاقتران الحُرّ ، التداعي الحرّ
analysis of dreams	تحليل الأحلام
slips of speech	زلّات الكلام ، زلّات اللسان
unconscious mind	العقل الباطن
early childhood experiences	خبرات الطفولة المبكرة
instinctual drives	دوافع غريزية
psychic energy	طاقة نفسية
defence mechanisms	حِيَل دفاعية
repression and regression	الكبت والنكوص
projection and sublimation	الإسقاط و الإعلاء

Exercise 1 . *Translate the previous passage into Arabic.*

Exercise 2. *Fill in this table with the suitable English derivatives whenever possible, and write down the Arabic equivalents of all the words.*

Verb		Noun		Adjective	
English	**Arabic**	**English**	**Arabic**	**English**	**Arabic**
develop					
derive					
				cognitive	
		approach			
				parental	
		evidence			
contribute					
		earning			
				moral	
		analysis			
				painful	
reveal					
		dream			
express					
		influence			
				conscious	
escape					

Exercise 3. *Translate these psychological terms:*

personality _____   ego _____

Id _____   superego _____

morals _____   values _____

attitudes _____   motives _____

instincts _____   feelings _____

emotions _____   ideals _____

UNIT 16

LAW AND POLITICS

Law VERSUS Power

INTERNATIONAL LAW, like the 'United Nations, is often treated in an all- or-nothing-at-all fashion. Either students of international politic put all of the delicate, fragile eggs of peace and security in to the basket of international law, or they assert that paramountcy of power re-duces the significance of international law in world politics to negli-gible proportions. The majority of textbooks on international relations leans toward the latter, "realist" view. Some of the works do not deal with international law at all, while many of them discuss it as per-forming a peripheral role in regulating relations among states . on the other hand, the "realists" dub as "idealists" those who urge substitution of the rule of law for the rule of force in world politics. For a time in the 1950's, this division between realists and "idealistic legalists" was particularly acute in the United States because of what was briefly called "The Great Debate on the National Interest."

The debate was initiated by students and practitioners of United states foreign relations, including Hans J. Morgenthau, the political scientist, and George Kennan, a career diplomat, who criticized the emphasis upon universalized democratic ideals and international law which, in their view, had been introduced into American foreign policy by Woodrow Wilson. They urged that the United States use its "*na- tional* interest" as the lode star of its foreign policy, instead of trying to make the world safe for democracy and from communism through observance of international law or through the attempted imposition of international law upon relations among states. At the time, each side to this argument was generally identified with fairly specific substan- tive foreign policies. Protagonists of the concept of national interest took a relatively "hard" line, defenders of Wilsonian idealism and logalism a relatively "soft" line on United States- Sovict relations. A decade later, however, these substantive positions had become blurred, especially on the side of the realists, where George Kennan and Hans J. Morgenthau favored more relaxed American postures vis-à-vis the communists. Kennan, the author of the policy of containment, could claim consistency in view of the loosening process that was taking place within what was not longer a monolithic communist "bloc." Mor- genthau, in his opposition to what he termed the overextension of American power in Southeast Asia, could claim consistency because of the redistribution of world power that followed the communist revolu-tion in China . Neither of them favored any heavier reliance upon in-ternational law or the United Nations in 1965 than in 1955. On the other side of the fence, advocates of "world peace through world law" thought that their claim to intellectual consistency was stronger than that of the realists, because they continued to couch their criticism of the foreign policies of their own or other governments in the same in-ternational-legal terms in the 1960's as in the 1950's For instance, they charged the United states with multiple violations of international law in Vietnam and Cuba, and the Soviet Union in Hungary or in the UN, over nonpayment of special assessments.

Because protagonists of international law and their critics in the Great Debate were identified with definite substantive foreign policies, the gulf between these two major schools of international relations was widened and the inadequacies of both approaches were made clearer.Both suffer from an excessively narrow and static conception of the origins, the functions, and the scope of law in political systems, and from false analogies of the role of law, so misconceived, in national states and international relations.

The "realists" return to what they consider the basic, crucial, and irreducible difference between these two levels of politics: presence and absence of a "sovereign," i.e., of some institution that can say the last word—by force, if necessary. Only if "law" is regularly observed, partly because of the possibility of enforcement, is it truly law. Within sovereign states, law is habitually observed, because it can be enforced and because most law is known to have been "made" by the sovereign.

Helpful Vocabulary :

international law	القانون الدولي
paramountcy of power	هيمنة القوة
negligible proportions	لا وزن لها نِسَب
world politics	السياسة العالمية
lean toward	تميل إلى
peripheral role	دور هامشي
rule of law	حُكْم القانون
rule of force	حُكْم القوة
idealistic legalists	القانونيون المثاليون
democratic ideals	المثل الديمقراطية
national interest	المصلحة القومية
observance of international law	الالتزام بالقانون الدولي
attempted imposition	محاولةُ فَرْض
Wilsonian idealism and legalism	المثالية الوِلْسُنيَّة والقانونية
vis-à-vis	فيما يتعلق بـِ
policy of containment	سياسة الاحتواء
communist bloc	الكتلة الشيوعية
overextension of power	بسط النفوذ
advocates of world peace	المدافعون عن السلام العالمي
schools of international relations	مذاهب في العلاقات الدولية
possibility of enforcement	إمكانية التنفيذ
for a time in the 1950's	لفترة في الخمسينيات من القرن العشرين

Exercise 1 . *Translate the previous passage into Arabic.*

Exercise 2. *Choose the proper preposition to fill in these   blanks : from, into, for, on, upon, for,   between, to, on ,with, on.*

1. Don't put all the eggs _____ one basket .

2. It can be reduced _____ zero .

3. This is a book _____ politics

4. It is difficult to deal _____ him

5. _____ the other hand, coeducation has many disadvantages .

6. The division _____ realists and idealist is a real one .

7. There was a hot debate _____ this issue last year .

8. The USA puts a great emphasis _____ the so-called national interests as a pretext _____ aggression.

9. How can we make our world safe _____ us all ?

10. Nowadays, millions of people suffer _____ AIDS .

Exercise 3. *Translate these political terms :*

party	_____	alliance	_____
coalition	_____	opposition	_____
rightist	_____	leftist	_____
policy	_____	plan	_____

UNIT 17

THE CENTRAL STATUS
OF LEARNING IN
PSYCHOLOGY

There are many branches and divisions of psychology and, while psychologists are engaged in many kinds of functions.There appears to be a basic agreement among them that the principles of learning are the fundamental theoretical tools of mod- ern psychology.

The science of psychology has developed around the S$\rightarrow$R formula in one modification or another. Organisms are presumed to rect in certain ways because they are stimulated into doing so. The reaction is either native or learned. If learned, it is because some stimulus which did not originally bring out a certain response now has come to do so because of "past experience" or "learning."

In civilized societies many natural reactions are found undesirable we frown on people who spit in the street or cough in our faces. The organism must not react "naturally" but in some other way, a way dictated by society. Attaching a different response to a stimulus is again "learning." From infancy on. the to-be-civilized human being is subjected to a training process calculated to make him an accept-able member of society. He is taught where and when to sleep, eat, wash behind the ears. read, write, and calculate, to earn his living, and even to grow old gracefully or die nobly, depending upon how the great divisions of society are getting along with each other at the time.

If the subject of all this training turns out delinquent, stupid, mal- adjusted, or otherwise a nuisance, it is usually assumed that the train- ing process went wrong somewhere, and retraining is usually recon- mended by the more enlightened segments of society.

Psychologists, in general, have adopted as their sphere of interest this process of training and retraining. Putting this interest in other terms, we can think of psychologists as basically concerned with the role of the environment in determining behavior. While there are exceptions. And many of them. most psychologists operate with the open avowal or tacit assumption that behavior can be predicted, con-trolled, or altered by manipulating the environment. This assump-tion, of course, is basic to many educational and child-rearing prac-tices.

The environmentalist bias was first put in its boldest form by John Locke (1690), the English philosopher, when he described the hu-man mind as a blank table on which experience would write the biography of the subject. Locke can be described as an "empiricist" as opposed to a "nativist." The nativists since Plato have held to the belief that humans, al least. come equipped by nature with some   basic ideas emotions, and reactions which are used on suitable oc-casions. The more extreme among them would endorse the common man's assertion, "you cant change human nature."

The history of psychology, to some extent, can be described in   terms of a controversy between supporters of "nature" as against "nurture." As with most black-white controversies, the searchers for   truth have found themselves forced to compromise from time to time   with occasional swings of the pendulum from one extreme to the   other.

The nature-nurture controversy still persists. In an interesting and disturbing article, Verplanck (1955) asked, "Since learned behavior is innate, and vice versa, what now?" This quotation, which is the title of his paper, expresses a question that is intriguing more and more psychologists since the publication of Hebb's (1949) mono-graph, the *organization* of *Behavior*.

Learning psychologists are beginning more and more to recognize   the role of the organism in behavior. Because of the nature of their tools and techniques they are pretty much limited to the manipula- tion of stimuli. The preoccupation with stimuli sometimes leads learning psychologists to forget about "nature" and act as if learning is all that matters.

It is basic to our needs to attempt an outcome which will place learning in its proper role in the total behavior pattern. Propaganda about how important learning is does not actually make it so, how-ever much it pleases the psychologist. In his presidential address to the American Psychological Association, Guthrie (1946a) states: "In the two fields of learning and of motivation will be worked out the   basic theory that will eventually make the science of psychology a much more powerful instrument than it now is. When we are able to state the general principles which govern human learning we shall have the most important tool needed for the prediction and control of human behavior. "Guthrie may be right.

Helpful Vocabulary :

modern psychology	علم النفس الحديث
S ⟶ R formula	صيغة المثير والاستجابة
native or learned reaction	ردّ فعل فطري أو مكتسَب
from infancy on	من الطفولة فصاعداً
training process	عملية تدريب
to earn his living	يكسب رزقه
to get along with each other	تنسجم مع بعضها البعض
enlightened segments	قطاعات مستنيرة
sphere of interest	مجال اهتمام
role of environment	دورة البيئة
child rearing	تنشئة الأطفال
determine behavior	يحدّد السلوك
blank tablet	لوحة فارغة
human nature	طبيعة الإنسان ، الفِطرة البشرية
nature against nurture	الفطرة ضد التربية
searchers for truth	الباحثون عن الحقيقة
compromise from time to time	يقبل بحل وسط من وقت لآخر
learning psychologists	علماء نفس التعلُّم
role of the organism	دور الكائن
manipulation of stimuli	التحكم بالمثيرات
process of training and retraining	عملية التدريب وإعادة التدريب
open avowal	إقرار صريح

82

Exercise 1 . *Translate the previous passage into Arabic.*

Exercise 2. *Fill in this table with the suitable English derivatives whenever possible,
and write down the Arabic equivalents of all the words.*

Verb		Noun		Adjective	
English	**Arabic**	**English**	**Arabic**	**English**	**Arabic**
engage					
		division			
appear					
		reaction			
				modern	
presume					
		response			
				civilized	
cough					
		stimulus			
				noble	
manipulate					
		extreme			
				graceful	
disturb					

Exercise 3. *Translate these psychological terms:*

Stimulus _____ response _____

habit _____ psychological clinic _____

psychological counseling _____

psychological development _____

psychological health _____

psychological maturity _____

psychological need _____

psychological test _____

UNIT 18

THE NATURE AND SCOPE OF PSYCHOLOGY

Nurses are increasingly aware of the need to base their actions on a sound knowledge of scientific principles. They have always made use of scientific knowledge derived from physiology and bacteriology. for example, but only in recent years have they discovered the relevance and usful-ness of the behavioural sciences, for example of psychology.

Many people use the term psychology very loosely. They do not really know what psychology is about and tend to confuse it with psychiatry, the study of mental disorder. Some people think that anyone who is good at coping with his fellow men is a psychologist. Some people are afraid of psychologists, believing that they have some special facility to see into the depths of that part of people's personality which they would prefer to conceal from others.

In the chapters which follow, it will become clear what psychology is really about and how nurses can use psycho- logical knowledge.

It is important to remember that knowledge of the subject matter does not make the reader a psychologist, any – more than knowledge of same basic physiology makes one a physiologist. Psychologists are scientists who, by the use of scientific research, push out the frontiers of psychological knowledge, which is then available for others to apply. Scientist construct theories based on objective facts derived from systematic observation and experiment.

Theories lead to hypotheses, which, after further observa- tion or experiment, will be confirmed or refuted, thus modi- fying the theories

In a young science, hypotheses are more frequently refuted than confirmed. What makes psychology a science is not that facts have been firmly established, but that the scientific method is applied to the subject matter to be studied .

Psychology is of interest to nurses because its subject matter is that of human behaviour. Nurses meet people every moment of their working day. The relationships with other, into which nurses enter in the course of their work, make the job interesting and rewarding. Some of the people the nurse meets may behave in a manner which is difficult to under-stand. Some may not be immediately likable. When the   nurse has taken the time and the trouble to try to understand such people's behaviour, she will find it much easier to gain cooperation and to deal effectively with the problems which may arise.

Human behaviour is only one part, however, of the sub- ject matter of psychology. Psychologists are also concerned with animal behaviour and with the neurophysiological pro-cesses which accompany or give rise to behaviour . They study not only human behaviour, but also human experience, language and other forms of communication they are in-terested in individual differences, be they genetically deter- minted or occurring as a result of learning, they study how individuals and society interact, how they behave as members of small and large groups.

No one psychologist can research into the entire range of the subject of psychology. The work of each psychologist must be restricted to one small section of the science. Some psychologists are concerned with the study of learning; some are interested in the phenomena of perception, namely the law which govern how stimuli arriving at the sense organs are interpreted into something meaningful, how past knowledge affects perception.

Some study the behaviour of animals; others are con- carned with the study of child behaviour or development; some are concerned with investigation of the effect of early childhood experiences; and others are interested in the inter-action of people with each other in small and large groups.

Helpful Vocabulary :

increasingly aware of	بشكل متزايد مدرك لِ
sound knowledge	معرفة سليمة
behavioral sciences	العلوم السلوكية
mental disorder	اضطراب نفسي
see into the depths	يَسْبِرُ أغْوارَ
push out the frontiers of	يوسِّع حدودَ
objective facts	حقوق موضوعية
systematic observation	ملاحظة منتظمة
theories and hypotheses	النظريات والفرضيات
confirm or refute	يؤكّد أو يرفض
young science	عِلمٌ حديث النشأة
firmly established facts	حقائق راسخة تماماً
human behavior	سلوك بشري
in the course of their work	في أثناء عملهنّ
subject matter of psychology	مادة علم النفس ، موضوع علم النفس
animal behavior	سلوك حيواني ، سلوك الحيوان
accompany or give rise to	تصاحب أو تثير
individual differences	الفروق الفردية
genetically determined	محددة وراثياً
be restricted to	يقتصر على
phenomena of perception	ظواهر الإدراك
sense organs	أعضاء الحسّ

Exercise 1 . *Translate the previous passage into Arabic.*

Exercise 2. *Fill in this table with the suitable English derivatives whenever possible, and write down the Arabic equivalents of all the words.*

Verb		Noun		Adjective	
English	**Arabic**	**English**	**Arabic**	**English**	**Arabic**
		nurse			
remember					
		need			
		use			
				loose	
derive					
		research			
				real	
refute					
				special	
		experiment			
confirm					
				systematic	
result					
				clear	
perceive					
		behavior			
				entire	

Exercise 3. *Translate these psychological terms:*

abnormal psychology	_____	child psychology	_____
adolescent psychology	_____	clininal psychology	_____
analytical psychology	_____	war psychology	_____
animal psychology	_____	comparative psychology	_____
applied psychology	_____	crowd psychology	_____

UNIT 19

GEOGRAPHY IN
AFTER-SCHOOL
LIFE

1. SOME knowledge of Geography is required from can-didates in many of the qualifying examinations held by the professional association, but as the possession of almost any kind of school Certificate exempts its holder from the professional preliminary tests of the associations of secretaries, accountants, and banking officials, there is no guarantee that the fully-fledged professional man shall have more than a slight acquaintance with the prin-ciples of Geography and their application to the work in which he is engaged. Judged by the syllabuses of these qualifying examinations, the majority of the professional associations regard Geography as being an essential ele- ment of school work, but with the exception of the Institutes of Banking, Insurance, and Transport. Geogra-phy is not included among the subjects which candidates may offer at subsequent examinations. It should be obvious, however, that many commercial posts require a detailed knowledge either of the industrial and commer- cial development of some particular area or of the manu-facturing and marketing of some specific commodity. In any case, a training in. Geography offers a valuable basis for the successful analysis of a given economic region and for its commercial exploitation. In the higher branches of secretarial practice, both commercial and political, a knowledge of economic and political Geography should associations concerned have refused to include Geography among the professional subjects.

2. Unfortunately it is not generally recognised that a

Knowledge of Geography is a necessary preliminary to the solution of many of the urgent problems which affect political and economic development throughout the world. At every stage of development there is a very definite need for the services of skilled geographers, ex- perts who able to survey the natural resources of a country and thereby to discover for what purposes each region is best suited, so that the maximum of production may be maintained. In certain countries steps have been taken to carry out the preliminary investigations which will lead to the establishment of reserves of land rich in timber and oil; but through the greater part of the world exploitation continues without consideration of the necessity of maintaining future supplies.

3. In addition to the practical application of geographical training to the everyday problems of economic and social development, there is a field of pure research. exploration, and survey which calls for special qualities of physical endurance, meticulous accuracy of observation and habits of mind which enable an individual to select and organize the data on which his judgments are based. An excellent example of the value of technical skill supported by a background of geographical knowledge is found in the work of the Ordnance Survey of Great Britain and the official survey departments of the colonies and protector-ates. The reputation for accurate work enjoyed by these institutions is such that, in a large number of cases of boundary limitation, the technical survey of the frontier to be established is carried out in collaboration . with British official survey officers.

4. In the past, political frontiers have been defined by politicians, lawyers, and soldiers, possessing little know- areas through which the boundaries they have fixed may pass. In many cases the results have been extremely unfortunate, and the political condition of Europe at the present time is largely the result of faulty frontier-making.

Helpful Vocabulary :

after –school life	حياة ما بعد المدرسة
qualifying examinations	امتحانات التأهيل
professional associations	جمعيات مِهْنية
school certificate	شهادة مدرسية
to exempt its holder from	يستثني حاملها مِنْ
no guarantee that	لا ضمانة أن
essential element	عنصر أساسي ، مكوّن جوهري
with the exception of	باستثناء
commercial posts	وظائف تجارية
detailed knowledge	معرفة تفصيلية
marketing of a commodity	تسويق سلعة
in any case	على أي حال
economic region	منطقة اقتصادية
commercial exploitation	الاستثمار التجاري
neverthess, hitherto	بالرغم من ذلك وحتى الآن
stages of development	مراحل التنمية
definite need	حاجة أكيدة
natural resources	موارد طبيعية
consideration of the necessity	مراعاة ضرورة
colonies and protectorates	المستعمرات والمحميات
boundary limitation	ترسيم الحدود
in collaboration with	بالتعاون مع

Exercise 1 . *Translate the previous passage into Arabic.*

Exercise 2. *Add a suitable preposition if necessary :*

1. it is required _____ you to know some facts .

2. There is no guarantee _____ that he will come back .

3. God does not judge you _____ your shape, but by your deeds.

4. _____ any case, you have to do what you have to do .

5. you may include this option _____ the other options .

6. Does X affect _____ Y ?

7. _____ addition, this factor may cause _____ a rise in prices

8. success calls _____ effort and persistence .

9. He has a good reputation _____ honesty .

10. He enjoys _____ a good skill .

Exercise 3. *Translate these worlds, showing two different meanings of each :*

kind	لطيف نوع	area	_____ _____
test	_____ _____	case	_____ _____
bank	_____ _____	branch	_____ _____
world	_____ _____	survey	_____ _____
subject	_____ _____	mind	_____ _____

UNIT 20

THE NEED FOR
MODELS

In the middle of the twentieth century there was a geography teacher who, because he was young, inexperienced and under- paid, was naturally expected to teach all branches of geography with equal knowledge and skill. His lectures on landforms, cyclones and soils were magnificent. He would enter the class-room looking forward to explaining a cycle of erosion or the process of leaching. His logical exposition was a delight to follow, and his multicoloured diagrams were a joy to behold. Many of his pupils, the girls included, were inspired to become geologists, meteorologists even soil scientists.

His lectures on the farming, manufacturing and the distribu-tion of population in different parts of the world were in-describably dull. Although he believed this part of geography to be the more interesting and important, his pupils endured the boredom, and went away convinced that human geography was just a matter of learning one damned fact after another. There was no logical exposition, there were no systems to illustrate by diagram, little to give any kind of intellectual stimulation and satisfaction.

Imagine, in another time and another place, this fictional geographer, perhaps older and shrewder, has specialised in the branch of human geography which preoccupies him most. For many years he has been dictating the facts of urban growth to student who couldn't care less: between 1951 and 1961 Manchester grew by so many thousand, Bradford by so many, and so on. By a mistake on the part of his employers he gets some time off to think, and he begins to wonder why these towns are growing, at exactly what rate they are growing, and whether all towns are growing at the same rate.

So the research geographer has a problem or question about the distribution and movement of people over a particular part of the earth's surface. His problem contains certain elements which will be essential to the discussion of models to be pursued in this book. Namely, he has certain phenomena. in this case the individuals of the population and the cities of different.

size; secondly there is some movement or interaction between the phenomena, in this case migration of people to cities. In fact he has tentatively identified what he believes to be a system on the earth's surface, and his aim is to describe and explain the functioning of that system as accurately as he can.

This geographer now follows the ideal course of action. Having observed some of the facts of a very complicated system, which is made infinitely more complicated by being inextricably interconnected with countless other systems, he proceeds to set up an hypothesis about the structure of the system and the way it works. Together with a *ver*bal description and explanation, this hypothesis may will take the form of a diagram to illustrate the structure. and ,mathematical equation to represent the functioning.

For the moment. Being interested only in the growth of towns, the elements of the system are defined as the native populations of the cities and the non-city population of the rest of the country. The growth of any city's population is then hypothesised as a function of both the size of the native popula- tion and the strength of the attraction of that city for the non-city population surrounding it. The geographer may decide to simplify and isolate further. in order to describe and understand one particular aspect of this. For agument's sake, he puts for-ward the hypothesis that the size of the migration to cities depends directly on the sizes of the cities; in other words, that a city of 1 million inhabitants attracts twice as many immi- grants as a city of 500 000 inhabitants over the save period of time

A diagram may be redundant in this example, but two things are essential: first, a mathematical equation to express the magnitude of migration to towns of different size, and secondly, a suggested or hypothetical explanation of why people behave in this manner. Such an explanation might run along the lines that many more people are attracted to they city of 1 million rather than the city of 500 000 because the former offers a greater variety of employment, a better chance of housing, a greater variety of shops and services, possesses colleges, theatres and other amenities which the other does not possess.

With his hypothetical diagram, equation and explanation, our geographer has crated a model of the real-life system he is studying. The model is a simplified hypothetical description and explanation of the interaction of phenomena on the earth's surface, and because the geographer is following the ideal course of action, his one aim in life is now to test his model. to test his hypothesis, until he proves it wrong. If this story were true, of course, he would simply select evidence to show that his hypothesis was a true description and explanation of what a actually happens in real life!

Helpful Vocabulary :

look forward to يتطلَّع إلى ، يتوق إلى

logical exposition عَرْض منطقي

soil scientists علماء التُّربة

distribution of population توزيع السكان

endured the boredom تحمل الملل

convinced that مقتنعون أنَّ

intellectual stimulation تحفيز ذهني

urban growth نموّ مديني ، نُمُوّ المدن

research geographer عالم الجغرافيا الباحث ، الجغرافيّ الباحث

interaction between phenomena تفاعل بين الظواهر

having observed … بعد أن لاحظ

verbal description وصف لفظيّ

mathematical equation معادلة رياضية

for the moment حالياً

non-city population السكان خارج المدن ، سكان غير المدن

native population السكان الأصليون

magnitude of migration حجم الهجرة

chance of housing فرصة إسكان

hypothetical description وصف افتراضي

his one aim هدفه الوحيد

to test the hypothesis يفحص الفَرْضيّة

put forward the hypothesis that يقدِّم فرضيةً مفادها أن

Exercise 1 . *Translate the previous passage into Arabic.*

Exercise 2. *Add the suitable preposition if necessary .*

1. He did it ——————— great skill .

2. He gave a lecture ——————— globalization .

3. Many ——————— the enjoyed the work .

4. They endured ——————— the boredom .

5. He has specialized ——————— medicine .

6. The city is growing ——————— a high rate .

7. ——————— this case, you have to do some more re-calculations .

8. ——————— the time being, he is the acting dean .

9. ——————— agument's sake, let us assume that he is not coming .

10. ——————— other words, heat causes expansion .

Exercise 3. *Translate these psychological terms :*

developmental psychology

————————————————

educational psychology

————————————————

experimental psychology

————————————————

functional psychology

————————————————

general psychology

————————————————

individual psychology

————————————————

industrial psychology

————————————————

occupational psychology

————————————————

UNIT 21

THE POLITICIAN'S
PROBLEM

The politician want power. Whether his intention is puplic service, or private gain, or private gain, or both, the first step is accession to a position of power: to be elected a Member of the Legislative Assembly. Broadly speaking there are three ways in which he can do the job. He may try to make a "mass contact"; he may use existing groups, nonpolitical as well as political; or, thirdly he may build up an organization of new groups.

To say that a politician his a "mass contact" is, in Orissa, to pay a high compliment. Such a man___and there are very few___has risen above the ordinary run of politicians who rely on cliques and factions for support. If a constituency con-sisted exclusively of the members of one caste and they all supported a candidate because he came from their caste, then, in the opinion of those with whom I discussed this question it would be wrong to call this "mass contact." An essential part of this relationship seem to be that it should transcend traditional loyalties.

Many difficulties stand in the way. The candidate who has a message for every household in his constituency has, in most cases, no means of delivering it. Secondly, even if he had the means, it would be difficult to compose a message which seemed constructive to everyone, still less a message that would please everyone.

Orissa has a population of over fourteen and on-half mil-lion (1951Census) and an Assembly of 140 members, one member to every 100,000 people. The area of the state is 60,000 square miles. Some constituencies are very large in area. particularly the rural double-member constituencies. The Assembly constituency in which Bisipara lay in the 1952 elec-tion covered 2,000 square miles; Keonjhar, in the district of the same name, covered 1,256 square miles; and Malkangiri in Koraput covered 2,288 square miles. The first two are double-member, and Malkangiri is a single-member constitu-ency. Only in those very few constituencies which consist of towns (for example Cuttack City covering 22 square miles) of which contain towns (like Puri) is the area small.

Size is not the only obstacle. Communications are bad-Even the ubiquitous jeep cannot reach many places and candi-dates must walk or, at best, use a bicycle. In western Orissa there are mountains and thick jungle; in the coastal plain there are many unbridged streams. Asuccessful candidate in Cuttack district canvassed all the major villages in his con-stituency. He travelled on foot and on cycle. He arrived in the afternoon in a village; addressd a meeting in the evening; in the morning he talked with those who showed interest and then moved on to the nest village. His constituency is not large__about 140 square miles, but the task took six months.

In more developed countries a politician can "put himself across" through the press, radio, and television. There is no television service and there are few radio sets in Orissa. As yet newspapers hardly reach the peasant. I have no figures for newspaper distribution, but one may make an estimate of their impact by looking at literacy figures. For the whole state literacy in Oriya is 15 pet cent; the highest rate is found in Cuttack (23 per cent); the lowest is in Koraput (5 per cent) Literacy is, of the press. A literate man in a village may share his pleasure by reading aloud to an audience. On the other hand not every literate man reads newspapers; nor are literates evenly spread through the population, for they tend to be concen-trated in the few towns. At least this may be safely said: up to now no politician in Orissa has been made or broken by what voters have read about him in the newspapers.

In short, a candidate who decides to treat his electors as a socially undifferentiated mass of rational minds, to be con-tacted and persuaded of the rightness of his cause, is not being realistic. He must find other means of communication

The Size of Vote-Banks

The candidate, therefore, has to take his electorate in groups. In a system which employs universal adult franchise it seems obvious that the larger the groups of voters, the better for the candidate who commands their allegiance.

Helpful Vocabulary :

public service	خدمة عامة
private gain	منفعة شخصية
accession to a position of power	الوصول إلى مركزِ سُلْطة
broadly speaking	بشكل عام
do the job	ينجز المهمَّة
Legislative Assembly	الجمعية التشريعية
mass contact	اتصال جماهيري
transcend traditional loyalties	تتجاوز الولاءات التقليدية
area of the state	مساحة الدولة
not the only obstacle	ليس العقبة الوحيدة
thick jungles	غابات كثيفة
at best	في أفضل الحالات
coastal plain	سهل ساحلي
unbridged streams	أنهار دون جسور
newspaper distribution	توزيع الجرائد
literacy figures	أرقام معرفة القراءة والكتابة
highest rate	النسبة العليا
high compliment	إطراء واسع
in most cases	في معظم الحالات
double-member	ذات عضوين
addressed a meeting	خاطب اجتماعاً
developed countries	بلدان متقدمة

Exercise 1 . *Translate the previous passage into Arabic.*

Exercise 2. *Fill in this table with the suitable English   derivatives whenever possible, and write down the Arabic equivalents of all the words.*

Verb		Noun		Adjective	
English	Arabic	English	Arabic	English	Arabic
intend					
		power			
deliver					
		contact			
		support			
				exclusive	
elect					
		compliment			
				constructive	
cover					
		tradition			
consist					
		place			
				distributed	
show					
		bridge			
				political	

Exercise 3. *Translate these pairs*

message ——————————— massage ———————————

faction ——————— fiction ———————

contact ——————— contract ———————

cm^2 ——————— cm^3 ———————

steam ——————— stream ———————

task ——————— tusk ———————

99

UNIT 22

THE FOUNDATIONS OF MODERN POLITICS

Whatever the world's political systems may have come to be in thirty years' time, the one thing certain is that they will be considerably unlike the systems under which most of us have been used to living. For better or worse we are in for comprehensive changes in the funda-mental structure of society ; and it will depend on us and on other men and women much like ourselves what is made of the objective conditions on which the States and societies of the future will have to be built. Of this we are one and all in varying degrees aware. We cannot help seeing that if we do not take part in shaping the society of to-morrow other people will shape it for us and we shall have to submit to the results of their political activity. Whether we play an active part or not, our lives and the lives of our children are being decided for us by the contentions of those who are active in a political sense. We can, if we wish, stand aside from the struggle at any rate for the moment, though we cannot be sure it will not forcibly drag us in before long. But even if we do stand aside we can by no possibility escape its consequences. For the political battle, while it assumes many different forms from place to place, is being carried on over the whole world, and there is no spot on earth to which a man can withdraw in the confidence that there at any rate it will pass him by and leave him to live his life unaffected. We are all in this thing up to the neck, however indifferent to it we may feel or wish to feel. It may matter little enough to us which political party controls the Government as long as the rival parties are divided only on minor issues and are at one in desiring to leave the essential structure of society intact. The position is very different when the questions at issue in politics go down to the very roots of human and social relationships, and the entire basis of our living together in society comes within the area of dispute.

Ours, then, is a political age. It is so in the main not because most of us want to be politically-minded but because we are being forced up against political problems by influences which we cannot escape. We have to shape things or let them be shaped for us by forces which we have renounced all attempt to control. To a certain extent these forces are impersonal, objective, material, and there is no getting away from them. But the shaping of human life within conditions set by these forces is a work for men, and if we play no part in to others will, and what they do will affect us. If we refuse to take an interest in politics to-day we are either cynics despairing of a world gone mad or less than intelligent human beings—mere living tools who will allow our future to be settled for us without making any attempt to control our fate.

Pre-war Politics. To most of us, who are old enough to remember the early years of the twentieth century, this new world of decisive political struggle still seems strange. Not that the existence of such a world is new, for in fact it is very old, but we have met with it until quite lately only in the history books and not in real life. For societies alternate between periods in which men jog along staidly, mounted upon political and social systems which it hardly occurs to most of them to question and, and periods in which men swop political horses, most often in the middle of the stream. It was the fortune of the nineteenth century to live through a period which, over most of the civilized world, combined an unprecedented rapidity of technical change with a remarkable stability of political and social institu-tions. Between 1789 and 1917 and, though the material face of civilization was changed beyond all recognition, not a single challenging new idea of primary political importance suc-ceeded in getting itself embodied in a practical shape. This was not because no new ideas were born. Socialism, for example, both came into being as a doctrine and took shape in a world-wide propagandist movement during the nineteenth century. But up to 1917, apart from the one short-lived local adventure of the pairs commune, Socialism was never able to express itself concretely in the institutions of any Socialist community. One idea of revolu-tion came to practical expression in France in 1789 and the following years, and thereafter the influence of that idea spread round the whole world. Socialism had to wait till 1917 to make its practical declaration of the *droits del' home et du citoyen* by means of an actual Socialist revolu-tion, and we are living to-day under the eye of that new declaration.

Helpful Vocabulary :

considerably unlike	مختلف جداً عن
for better of worse	سواء أكان للأفضل أم للأسوأ
fundamental structure	التركيبة الأساسية
objective conditions	ظروف موضوعية
one and all	فرادى ومجتمعين
of this... aware	لهذا ... مدركون
active part	دور نَشيط
for the moment	مؤقتاً
before long	قبل مرور وقت طويل
escape consequences	يتجنب النتائج
being carried on	تستمر
pass him by	تتعداه ، تتجاوز
may matter little	قد يهمّ قليلاً
rival parties	أحزاب متنافسة
minor issues	مشكلات صغرى
are at one	متحدون
area of dispute	منطقة نزاع
so in the main	هكذا بشكل رئيسي
shape things	نشَّكل الأشياء ، نصوغ الأشياء
no getting away from them	لا مهرب منها
to a certain extent	إلى حدٍ ما
politically-minded	مُسَيَّسٌ عقلياً ، ذو عقل مُسَيَّس

102

Exercise 1 . *Translate the previous passage into Arabic.*

Exercise 2. *Add the suitable preposition if necessary : of ,   for , from , to , for , to , in , to , on .*

1. ——————— Better or worse, change is coming .

2. He depend ——————— his parents .

3. They are aware ——————— dangers .

4. You must take part ——————— the plan .

5. If you do not decide, someone will decide ——————— you .

6. I'm sure ——————— that he'll come.

7. It differs ——————— place ——————— place .

8. This is true ——————— a certain extent .

9. Time does not await ———————the lazy .

10. Such a thing has never occurred ———————me .

Exercise 3. *Translate these words, showing their meanings   as verbs and nouns :*

help	مساعدة	يساعد	spot	———	———
change	———	———	leave	———	———
play	———	———	matter	———	———
wish	———	———	dispute	———	———
battle	———	———	shape	———	———

UNIT 23

THINKING ABOUT

POLITICS

MANY PEOPLE have only a vague idea of what is meant by the term "political science." Often they confuse it with politi-cal economy, which is economics; or they conceive it to be the discussion of current events, although there is no more reason for a political scientist to know offhand the present situation in the Near East than for a professor of physical machanics to be able to describe the pilings of any bridge in North Carolina. They often believe that political science is civic ethics, that is, a system of moral exhortations that tell student what is good and bad about the political conduct of various presons and groups .

Political science is fundamentally none of these things. It is scientific method applied to political events. Like any other science, it is an attempt to reduce, by ever-broader state-ments, the facts with which it deals to a number of clear, precise, descriptive principles. Of course, in a science called political, these facts and principles are political. A principle of political science might be: "Third parties have a difficult time getting on the ballot in most states"; or "The system of filling committee chairmanships by seniority in the Congress operates on the whole to the advantage of the conservative Southern faction of the Democratic party when that party is in the majority."

The Science and Art of Politics

POLITICS IS AN ART

However confused some people may be about political science, they seem to have clear-cut and dogmatic ideas about politics. To many voters, politics is a racket, a game, or a disgrace; but to those they elect to office, who are "in poli-tics," it may be a noble profession. Such epithets, however can only express emotional reactions, not the realities of politics. Practical politics actually resolves itself into the ad-justments of human relations. It calls for a practical skill that distinguishes one man from another——an art. Long training, even if only self-training or experience, elevates one man above another, and when training and aptitude increase a skill, we have conditions that are typical of an art, whether it be bad or good, plain or fancy art. A few men seem to be born to the political art.

Science presents the principles: the corresponding art applies them. So, in theory, should the political scientist pro-vide the principles for the political artist—the politician, the administrator, the active citizen. It would be false, however, to conceal the fact that the co-ordination between the scientist and the politician, in practice, is slight.

This situation is by no means peculiar to political science. Knowing the principles of anatomical mechanics hardly helps one walk better, and he who trys consciously to operate by them may well fall on his face. On the other hand, without a science of anatomy and engineering, artificial limbs could not be employed successfully. Even in those areas where science and art are indispensable to one another, co-ordination can-not be perfect. The engineer learns mechanics in school and even takes courses in the art of bridge building, that is, "applied" courses; but he does not learn how to build *the* bridge of real life. The bridge is unique; it is his individual solution of a special bridging problem—a problem of scien-tific principle, aesthetic principle, climate, public opinion, and perhaps even politics.

POLITICS AND COMMON SENSE

Certainly, to the neutral observer and to the artist of poil-tics the political world seems so confused and complex that most of the descriptions of it over the last two thousand years appear to be monstrous oversimplifications, completely use-less as guides for political practical practice. Everything seems to be done according to homely sayings that people have ac-quired during their individual life experiences or by reason of some complex "feeling" for the particular situation that cannot be broken down into a statement of scientific principle or taught to others. When one asks a politician whether there are principles of political science that underlie his activities, he snorts in derision or else emits several heavy dogmas that he would never in his right mind pursue implacabley: "Never offend anybody;" Always vote for appropriations and against taxes;" "Be loyal;" or "God is on the side with the most votes. "

105

Helpful Vocabulary :

vague idea   فكرة غامضة

political science   علم السياسة

civic ethics   علم الأخلاق المدني

political events   الأحداث السياسة

committee chairmanships   رئاسات اللجان

by seniority   بالأقدمية

on the whole   بشكل عامّ

in the majority   له الأغلبية

to many voters   في نظر كثير من المصوّتين

emotional reactions   ردود فعل عاطفية

in theory   نظرياً

in practice   عملياً

on the other hand   من ناحية أخرى

science of anatomy   علم التشريح

artificial limbs   الأطراف الاصطناعية

indispensable to one another   لا غنى لأي منهما عن الآخر

bridge building   بناء الجسور

aesthetic principle   مبدأ جمالي

public opinion   الرأي العامّ

to the neutral observer   بالنسبة للمراقب المحايد

monstrous oversimplification   إفراط كبير في التبسيط

political practice   الممارسة السياسية

in his right mind   وهو سليم العقل

Exercise 1 . *Translate the previous passage into Arabic.*

Exercise 2. *Fill in this table with the suitable English derivatives whenever possible, and write down the Arabic equivalents of all the words.*

Verb		Noun		Adjective	
English	**Arabic**	**English**	**Arabic**	**English**	**Arabic**
confuse					
				vague	
conceive					
		discussion			
				present	
bridge					
		group			
				conservative	
vote					
		advantage			
resolve					
		professor			
				peculiar	
distinguish					
		art			
				complex	
simplify					
		problem			

Exercise 3. *Translate these pairs*

involve	_____	revolve	_____
elect	_____	select	_____
human	_____	humane	_____
must	_____	a must	_____
face	_____	phase	_____

UNIT 24

THE ART OF LITERATURE

LITERATURE is an art by which ex-pression is achieved in language. As a pre-liminary description, that statement will do well enough; but it is evidently inade-quate as a definition of literature . Not everything which might come under that description would be called literature——not at least, if the word literature is to retain any precision of meaning : and when we allow a word to become vague in its mean-ing, we deprive it of its usefulness. Thus, conversation is not literature; and yet we speak of the art of conversation. The word *art*, in fact, appears to have many mean-ings : besides the so-called fine arts, we speak of the art of cooking, the art of war, the art of advertising, and a hundred other art. But the word has the same core of meaning in all its contexts : it is always skill definitely and deliberately designed to produce an intended result. Clearly, then we cannot rely on the word *art* to define what we mean by literature; if we at-tempted to do so, we should only beg the question, and say, in effect, that art here means the art which produces literature On the contrary, we can only define what we mean by art here when we know what we mean by literature. Certainly, there are degrees of skill; we may easily admit that in literature there is a degree of verbal skill ⸺more studied, more con-sistent, more intent ⸺than in conversa- *only* in words : in conversation. the skill is also in the use of personality ⸺sometimes more than in the use of words. Poetry may be recited, of course, and plays may be acted ; but the literary art is substantially the same whether it is spoken aloud or read in silence.

We must not, therefore, define literature by referring it to the written or printed or printed word. For the word intelligible to the eye is only the symbol of the word intelligible to the ear ; and is in fact *heard* (though it may be only mentally) at the same time that it is visually read. Moreover, in a great deal of literature⸺in all poetry, for instance⸺it is as essential to the art of it that the words should be vividly heard (though, once more, they need be only mentally heard) as that they should be understood.

Precisely what we mean by art in the case of literature, then, must be left to appear as we narrow . down the idea of literature. Art, we say, is skill designed to produce an intended result. What is the result aimed at in the art of literature ? we have described literature as a species of expression. But this is only one side of the business. Literature exists not only in expressing a thing; it equally exists in the receiving of the thing expressed. If I tell you of something I have experienced my words, on my side, *express* my experience ; but on your side, my words *represent* my experience.

Helpful Vocabulary :

preliminary description	وصف مبدئيّ ، وصف أوليّ
evidently inadequate	من الواضح غير كافية
precision of meaning	دقة المعنى
art of conversation	فن المحادثة
the so-called fine arts	ما يدعى الفنون الجميلة
intended result	نتيجة مقصودة
we beg the question	ندور في حلقة مفرغة
in effect	نتيجة لذلك
on the contrary	على العكس
degrees of skill	درجات من المهارة
read in silence	يقرأ قراءة صامتة
printed word	الكلمة المطبوعة
word intelligible to the eye	كلمة تدركها العين
word intelligible to the ear	كلمة تدركها الأذن
mentally heard	تسمع ذِهنياً
easily admit	يعترف بسهولة
and yet	ومع ذلك
art of advertising	فن الإعلان

110

Exercise 1. *Translate the previous passage into Arabic.*

Exercise 2. *Fill in this table with the suitable English derivatives whenever possible, and write down the Arabic equivalents of all the words.*

Verb		Noun		Adjective	
English	**Arabic**	**English**	**Arabic**	**English**	**Arabic**
achieve					
		literature			
				evident	
state					
		word			
				easy	
retain					
		precision			
deprive					
		war			
mean					
		cooking			
				peculiar	
attempt					
		context			
				intelligible	
product					

Exercise 3. *Translate these pairs :*

intend	_____	attend	_____
define	_____	refine	_____
big	_____	beg	_____
produce	_____	product	_____
refer	_____	defer	_____
fact	_____	factual	_____

111

UNIT 25

LIFE AND WRITINGS OF
ARISTOTLE

Aristotle was born in 384/3 B.C. at Stageira in Thrace, and was the son of Nicomachus, a physician of the Macedonian king, Amyntas II. When he was about seventeen years old Aristotle went to Athens for purposed of study and became a member of the Academy in 368/7 B.C., where for over twenty years he was in constant intercourse with Plato until the latter's death in 348/7 B.C. He thus entered the Academy at the time when Plato's later dialectic was being developed and the religious tendency was gaining ground in the great philosopher's mind. Probably already at this time Aristotle was giving attention to empirical science (i.e. at the time of Plato's death) , and it may be that he had already de-parted from the Master's teaching on various points; but there can be no question of any radical break between Master and pupil as long as the former was still alive. It is impossible to suppose that Aristotle could have remained all that time in the Academy had he already taken up a radically different philosophical position to that of his Master. Moreover, even after Plato's death Aristotle still uses the first person plural of the representatives of the Platonic doctrine of Ideas, and soon after Plato's death Aristotle eulo-gises him as the man "whom bad men have not even the right to praise, and who showed in his life and teachings how to be happy and good at the same time." The notion that Aristotle was in any real sense an opponent of Plato in the Academy and that he was a thorn in the side of the Master, is scarcely tenable: Aristotle found in Plato a guide and friend for whom he had the greatest admiration, and though in later years his own scientific interests tended to come much more to the fore, the metaphysical and reli-gious teaching of Plato had a lasting influence upon him. In-deed, it was this side of Plato's teaching that would have perhaps a special value for Aristotle, as offsetting his own bent towards empirical studies.

After Plato's death Aristotle left Athens with Xenocrates (Sepusippus, Plato's nephew, had become head of the Academy, and with him Aristotle did not see eye to eye; in any case he may not have wished to remain in the Academy in a subordinate position under its new head), and founded a branch of the Academy at Assos in the Troad. Here he influenced Hermias, ruler of Atarneus, and married his niece and adopted daughter, Pythias. While working at Assos, Aristotle no doubt began to develop his own in-dependent views. Three years later he went to Mitylene in Lesbos, and it was there that he was probably in inter-course with Theophrastus, a native of Eresus on the same island, who was later the most celebrated disciple of Aris-totle. (Hermias entered into negotiations with Philip of Macedon, who conceived the idea of an Hellenic defeat of the Persians. The Persian general, Mentor, got hold of Hermias by treachery and carried him off to Susa, where he was tortured but kept silence. His last message was:"Tell my friends and companions that I have done nothing weak or unworthy of philosophy." Aristotle published a poem in his honour.)

In 343/2 Aristotle was invited to Pella by Philip of Macedon to undertake the education of his son Alexander, then thirteen years old. This period at the court of Macedon and the endeavour to exercise a real moral influence on the young prince, who was later to play so prominent a part on the political stage and to go down to posterity as Alexander the Great, should have done much to widen Aristotle's hori-zon and to free him from the narrow conceptions of the ordinary Greek, though the effect does not seem to have been so great as might have been expected: Aristotle never ceased to share the Greek view of the City-State as the centre of life. When Alexander ascended the throne in now presumably at an end, and probably went for a time to Stageira, his native city, which Alexander rebuilt as payment of his debt to his teacher.

Helpful Vocabulary :

Macedonian king	ملك مقدونيا
in costant intercourse with	في اتصال دائم بـِ
the latter's death	موت الأخير
religious tendency	الميل الديني
was giving attention	كان يعطي اهتماماً
empirical science	العلم التجريبي
departed form	افترق عن ، نأى عن
radical break	انفصال كبير ، اختلاف جذري
had he taken up	لو أنه اتخذ
eulogise him	يَرْثيه
opponent of Plato	خَصْم لأفلاطون
thorn in his side	شوكة في خاصرته
lasting influence	تأثير دائم
break to pieces	يتحطَّم
under the weight of facts	تحتَ وطأةِ الحقائق
up to now	حتى الآن
did not see eye to eye	لم يره وجهاً لوجهٍ
founded a branch	أسَّس فرعاً
his adopted daughter	ابنته المتبنَّاة
independent views	آراء مستقلة
disciple of Aristotle	تلميذ أرسطو
Hellinic defeat	هزيمة هلينية

Exercise 1 . *Translate the previous passage into Arabic.*

Exercise 2. *Fill in this table with the suitable English derivatives whenever possible, and write down the Arabic equivalents of all the words.*

Verb		Noun		Adjective	
English	**Arabic**	**English**	**Arabic**	**English**	**Arabic**
		purpose			
				old	
use					
praise					
		dialectic			
				radical	
admire					
		position			
				good	
		opponent			
				real	
expect					
		side			
				thorny	
head					
		friend			
				scare	
celebrate					

Exercise 3. *The suffix -ism is added to adjectives to make abstract nouns, usually referring to philosophies or trends. Translate these terms :*

Platonism _____   globalism _____

modernism _____   imperialism _____

extremism _____   idealism _____

existentialism _____   fundamentalism _____

UNIT 26

ANCIENT PHILOSOPHY

1.   SCIENTIFIC interest in ancient, especially in Greek, philosophy, is not confined to the value that it possesses as a peculiar subject for historical research and for the study of the growth of civilization. But it is also equally con-cerned in the permanent siguificance that the content of ancient thought possesses by reason of its place in the development of the intellectual life of Europe.

The emphasis falls primarily upon the lifting of mere knowing to. the plane of systematic knowledge, or science. Not content with his storing of practical facts, and with his fantastic speculations born of his religious needs, the Greek sought knowledge for its own sake. knowledge, like art, was developed as an independent function from its involvement in the other activities of civilization. So, first and foremost, the history of ancient philosophy is *an insight into the origin of European science in general.*

It is, however, at the same time the history of the birth of the separate sciences, for the process of differentia-tion, which begins with distinguishing thought from con-duct and inythology, was continued within the domain of science itself. With the accumulation and organic ar-rangement of its facts, the early, simple, and unitary science to which the Greeks gave the name $\phi\iota\lambda_{o\sigma}o\phi$ *lai,* and these then continued to develop on more or less independent lines.

Concerning the history and meaning of the name of "phi-losophy, "see especially R. Haym, in Ersch and Gruber's *Eney-klopudie*, III. division, vol. 24; Ueberweg, *Grundriss*, I. I; Windelband, *Praeludien*, P. 1 ff. The word became a technical tern in the Socratic school. It meant there exactly what sci-ence , the word philosophy had the sense of ethicho-religious practical wisdom. See 2.

The beginnings of scientific life that are thus found in ancient philosophy are most influential upon the entire development that follows. With proportionately few data,Greek philosophy produced, with a kind of grand simplicity conceptual forms for the intellectual elaboration of its facts, and with a remorseless logic it developed every essential point of view for the study of the universe. Therein con-sists the peculiar character of ancient thought and the high didactic significance of its history. Our present language and our conception of the world are thoroughly permeated by the results of ancient science. The naïve ruggedness with which ancient philosophers followed out single motives of reflection to their most one-sided logical conclusions brings into elearest relief the practical and psychological necessity which governs not only the evolution of the problems of philosophy, but also the repeated historical tendencies toward the solution of these problems. We may likewise ascribe a typical significance to the universal stages of development of ancient philosophy, in view of the fact that philosophy at first turned with undaunted courage to the study of the outer world; thwarted there, it turned back to the inner world, and from this point of view, with renewed strength, it attempted to conceive the World-All. Even the manner in which ancient thought placed its entire apparatus of conceptual knowledge at the service of social and religious needs has a peculiar and more than historical value.

The real significance of ancient philosophy will be much ex-aggerated if one tries to draw close analogies between the dif-ferent phases of modern philosophy and its exponents, and those of the ancients. Read K. v. Reichin-Meldegg, *D. Paral-lelismus d. alten u neuen Philosophie*, Leipzig and Heidelberg, 1865. A detailed parallelism is impossible, because all the forms of the modern history of civilization have so much more nearly complete presuppositions, and are more complicated than those of the ancient world. The typical character of the latter is valid in so far as they have "writ large' and often nearly grotesquely the simple and elemental forms of mental life, which among moderns are far more complicated in their combinations.

Helpful Vocabulary :

not confined to	ليست مقصورة على
historical research	بحث تاريخي
growth of civilization	تطور الحضارة
content of ancient thought	محتوى الفكر القديم
intellectual life	الحياة الفكرية
mere knowing	مجرّد المعرفة
not content with	غير قانع بـ
first and foremost	أولاً وقبل كل شيء
domain of science	مجالُ العلم
process of differentiation	عملية التَّمايُز
accumulation of facts	تراكم الحقائق
Socratic school	المدرسة السقراطية ، مدرسة سقراط
ethico-religious practical wisdom	حكمة عملية أخلاقية دينية
most influential on	مؤثر جداً على
grand simplicity	بساطة رائعة
point of view	وجهة نظر
peculiar character	سِمَة مميّزة ، سِمَة خاصّة
conception of the world	إدراك العالَم
historical tendencies	ميول تاريخية
stages of development	مراحل التطور
not only ... but also ...	ليس فقط ... بل أيضاً ...
motives of reflection	دوافع التأمُّل ، دوافع التفكير

118

Exercise 1 . *Translate the previous passage into Arabic.*

Exercise 2. *Add the suitable preposition if necessary:* in , into , upon ,
toward , for , to , into , to , in , with , to

1. He has great interest _____ science .

2. Factionalism has been a good reason _____civil_____ war in that
   country .

3. Research has succeeded _____ lifting mythology
   up _____ the level of science .

4. This requires some insight _____ the case .

5. philosophy later was divided _____ separate

6. Islam has a great influence _____ Muslims .

7. As a father, he always treats his children _____ a lot
   of mercy .

8. The tendency _____ globalization may prove to be very
   dangerous _____ small countries .

9. His success may be ascribed _____ his hard work .

10. Let bygones be _____ bygones .

UNIT 27

INDUSTRIAL SOCOETY AND INDEUSTRIAL SOCIOLOGY

Probably the outstanding characteristic of contemporary West-ern societies is that they have been forced into a situation where change is a constant phenomenon. So dynamic is this pattern of change that it is irresistibly spreading to the entire world. Usually the change is conceived as emanating from persistent. Techno-logical innovations which come to constitute a cultural pattern.

While such an explanation is grossly correct, it is an oversim-plification, for technological innovation are accompanied, if not preceded, by changes in values and social organization. It is not an exaggeration to suggest that the so-called industrial revolution was accompanied from the very beginning by an organizational revolution, and that both accompanied a change in value systems. Today the revolutions in technology, organization, and values are constantly altering both traditional and industrial societies.

It is often overlooked that the revolution in manufacturing which gained impetus in eighteenth-century western Europe was preceded by changes in the values of the societies that composed it. While many different values became modified, the underlying change was the invasion of rational though into many areas pre-viously considered sacred. The area which felt the greatest ap-plication of rational systems of though was economics, particu-larly in manufacturing. In an interdepedndent society all other social institutions had to make corresponding adjustments. In this particular sense. We can think of the industrial revolution as creating an industrial society. The general purpose of industrial sociology is to study this broad process of industrialization and its impact on various segments of the society by the application of general sociological principles.

It is strange that industrial sociology emerged in the United states at a tine when the number of people engaged in manu-facturing was surpassed by the number employed in nonmanufacturing or service industries. Although less than a quarter of its population is currently occupied in manufacturing the United States, like several western European countries, is a mature indus-trial society. Apparently the structures of industrializing societies exhibit a predictable pattern; the number of people engaged in manufacturing increases until it surpasses the number engaged in agriculture. At a further stage, the proportion of workers em-ployed in the so-called service (nonmanufacturing) industries exceeds that of workers in manufacturing while the proportion engaged in agriculture continues to decline. Obviously this con-dition would be impossible without an increasingly efficient sys-tem of manufacturing which can support a growing number of workers in "nonproduction" industries. Thus, although a minor-ity of workers may be employed in manufacturing industries, it is possible to have an industrialized economy. Moreover, the economy may be characterized as "industrial" in the sense that nonmanufacturing work organizations increasingly model their values and structures after manufacturing organization. Marker-ing, wholesaling, retailing, transportation. Communication, edu-cation, health care, banking, and other services are becoming "factories" in marketing, wholesaling, retailing, transportation, communication, education, and so on.

the impact of the industrial complex manifests itself also in the nonindustrial or noneconomic realm. That is to say, other institutions of the society respond to the demands and needs of the economic institutions, and this seems to be the case irrespec-tive of the pattern of property ownership found in the society-

To be sure, although other institutions do have an impact on the functioning of the economy, the reverse process, as Polanyi suggests, tends to be general in industrial societies. Thus one of the main functions of government is to control the economy; one of the main problems of education is to train people for technical and other roles in the economy; one of the main functions of the family is to socialize individuals for living in this type of econ-omy; one of the main problems of religion is to reinterpret life meanings to people who are exposed to the economic instabilities; and the main task of welfare is to provide for those cast adrift by the malfunctions of the economy.

Helpful Vocabulary :

outstanding characteristic	سمة بارزة
contemporary societies	مجتمعات معاصرة
constant phenomenon	ظاهرة دائمة
technological innovations	ابتكارات تقَانيَّة
social organization	تنظيم اجتماعي
value systems	الأنظمة القَيميَّة
traditional societies	مجتمعات تقليدية
western Europe	أوروبا الغربية
rational thought	الفكر العقلاني
interdependent society	مجتمع متبادل الاعتماد
corresponding adjustments	تكيُّفات مماثلة
industrial sociology	علم الاجتماع الصناعي
process of industrialization	عملية التصنيع
service industries	صناعات خِدْميَّة
occupied in manufacturing	منخرطون في التصنيع
predictable pattern	نمط قابل للتنبؤ
continue to decline	يستمر في الهبوط
nonproduction industries	صناعات غير إنتاجية
wholesaling	البيع بالجملة
irrespective of	بغضّ النظر عن
efficient system	نظام كفء
in the sense that	بمعنى أنَّ

Exercise 1 . *Translate the previous passage into Arabic.*

Exercise 2. *Fill in this table with the suitable English derivatives whenever possible, and write down the Arabic equivalents of all the words.*

Verb		Noun		Adjective	
English	**Arabic**	**English**	**Arabic**	**English**	**Arabic**
force					
		phenomenon			
				western	
emanate					
		change			
				resistible	
simplify					
		innovation			
				persistent	
		exaggeration			
compose					
				industrial	
		revolution			
modify					
		segment			
				sacred	
surpass					

Exercise 3. *The suffix -ism is added to adjectives to make verbs. Translate these words :*

europeanize   _____   islamize   _____

westernize   _____   globalize   _____

americanize   _____   italianize   _____

anglicize   _____   jordanize   _____

arabize   _____   nationalize   _____

UNIT 28

RESEARCH IN THE SOCIOLOGY OF EDUCATION

The purpose of this collection of papers is to present evidence of the contemporary contribution of research in the sociology of education to the understanding of education and of society. The output of research in the sociology of education is probably greater and certainly as great as that in any field of sociology. In the past decade support from the research foundations has been generous and the number of individual studies has increased rapidly. Yet the contribution of this output has been minimized by a concentration of attention on a limited range of widely quoted studies; by a theoretical orientation that is implicit rather than explicit and, at times, an excessive and distorting use of its findings by pressure groups. Notwithstanding these problems, however, the potential contribution of findings from research in the sociology of education is considerable, and increasingly decisions on such matters as school organization, teachers' roles, curriculum content and the like are made in the belief that they are supported, or at least legitimated, by sociologically oriented research. The fact that such legitimation may be assumed rather than actual presents a further justification for the publication of his collection which, it is hoped, will help to reduce the uncertainties and uninformedness about the nature and standing of research in the field and draw attention to the complex interrelationship between educational research and policy. It is not a guide for those who wish to produce educational research; but rather a guide for those who seek access to the intellectual and emotion-all core of research and, in so doing, wish to use it critically.

The collection contains a range of research studies that include a number that have not been published previously and others that have been virtually unobtainable outside their countries of origin (France, Finland and Sweden). A consideration of their context, content and contribution forms the remainder of this general introduction to the volume; there are also specific editorial introductions to the various sections of the book in which the individual papers are discussed

A dominant feature of the context of all contemporary research in the sociology of education is the controversy between scientific positivism and the reaction to it, notably from phenomenological and ethnomethodological approaches; the 'normative' and 'interpretative' perspectives. Alongside this there is the closely related conflict between 'value free' and 'value oriented' sociology.

Both of these conflicts are central to the nature of research and its understanding and use. But they are conflicts which dominate sociology as a whole and not just the sociology of education. Accordingly it is necessary to consider briefly the condition of sociological research generally before exploring the particularly educational connotations or research in the discipline.

The establishment of sociological research

'pure' research in sociology is currently beset by a paradox; it has become both established and disestablished more or less concurrently. The establishment is unquestionable-recognition in universities and colleges throughout most of the world for sociology as a subject with academic standing and with legitimate research functions; a rapid growth in the range of accredited and well-funded research institutes; definitive recognition through direct sponsorship from major funding organizations and through public grant-awarding bodies.

The establishment of research in sociology has been a necessary condition of the establishment of the discipline itself. Only by demonstrating, empirically, that there are laws governing human behaviour in societies could sociology substantiate its claim for a legitimate separate existence either from literature with its established capacity to describe and interpret human interaction, or from history with its established strategies of analyzing unique events and their consequences. The battle for scientific recognition of this kind was first fought by the psychologists, successfully but at considerable cost to the development of the subject-where the crudities of behaviourism, having the manner of approved scientific method, were tolerated, while the exciting but largely untestable hypotheses in the field of psycho-analysis presented continuous embarrassment. The rigorous formalism of the British Psychological Society, still largely modelled on the prestigious pure science organizations, points to a continuing belief in a need for scientific respectability.

Sociology was spared some of these traumas. The recognition of psychology opened the path for the recognition of sociology even though it was along a path that had been laid down by the psychologists. But at least some of the exertions to establish it could be avoided by sociologists who were able to devote somewhat more of their time to exploring sociological as opposed to scientific perspectives. In this they were helped by the standing of anthropological study as a distinct and acceptable even if somewhat remote area of study. Yet the influence of the psychological interpretation of the pure science model on sociology is regularly to be seen, and Swift (1973) has noted that sociologists in Britain still find themselves 'forced into doing social psychology. He suggests that many of the problems in the way of a fruitful relationship between sociology and psychology spring from the psychologically determined path of recognition that has had to be trodden by sociologists. There are many examples in present day sociology that reaffirm this history. The almost universal use of Durkheim's Suicide[2] and the compulsory statistical course, both of which form part of the routine socialization of first year sociology undergraduates, and the disfavor with which 'applied' social work students are often viewed. are well-known phenomena.

Helpful Vocabulary :

to present evidence	يقدم الدليل
sociology of education	علم الاجتماع التربوي
output of research	مُخرَجات البحث
research foundations	مؤسسات البحوث
concentration of attention	تركيز الاهتمام
at times	في بعض الأوقات
pressure groups	جماعات الضغط
curriculum content	محتوى المنهج
further justification	تبرير إضافي
educational research and policy	البحث التربوي والسياسات
countries of origin	بلدان المنشأ
editorial introduction	مقدّمة المحرّر
scientific positivism	الوضعية العلمية ، اليقينية العلمية
normative perspective	منظور معياري
interpretive perspective	منظور تفسيري
"value-free" society	مجتمع خالٍ من القيم
"value-oriented" society	مجتمع مهتم بالقيم
grant-awarding bodies	هيئات مانحة
academic standing	مكانة أكاديمية
accredited institutes	معاهد معترف بها
legitimate existence	وجود مشروع
untestable hypotheses	فرضيات غير قابلة للفحص

Exercise 1 . *Translate the previous passage into Arabic.*

Exercise 2. *Give the Arabic equivalents of these groups of   words, each of which belongs to the same   semantic field :*

1. paper _____ series _____

   thesis _____ volume _____

   dissertation _____ newspaper _____

   book _____ magazine _____

   booklet _____ periodical _____

   pamphlet _____ encyclopedia _____

2. education _____ master _____

   teaching _____ pupil _____

   Instruction _____ student _____

   curriculum _____ full professor _____

   Teacher _____ assistant professor _____

   instructor _____ associate professor _____

3. research _____ table _____

   researcher _____ diagram _____

   proposal _____ footnote _____

   plan _____ appendix _____

   contents _____ bibliography _____

UNIT 29

THE NATURE OF SOCIETY

WHEREVER there are mien they are found to be living in societies. The simpler peoples, such as the Eskimos, or the Veddahs, or the Andaman Islanders, are commonly found in small groups, which may range in size from thirty or forty to a few hundred individuals. But for the most part human societies are larger than that. It is true that there may be found individuals who have lived with very little contact with other human being ; there are many well-authenticated stories of children who have been carried off and reared by wild animals ; there are other well-authenticated stories of children reared in solitary confinement ; and there are adults who become separated from their kind, castaways and prisoners and recluses. But such men and women art exceptional, and usually they appear to be damaged by solitude. In the case of those individuals who have been carried off n childhood there is always, for obvious reasons, defective development; to become a human being, in any adequate sense of that term, it is not sufficient to have been born of human stock, it is also necessary to have grown up in a human society and to have been subjected to its influences.

Those influences are of many kinds and of great power. The ordinary man does not, as a rule, realize the extent to which his thinking, his feeling, and his behaviour are likely to be social products. It seems to him that he thinks and that he feels as he does because it is natural and right to think and to feel in those ways, and that he behaves as he does because he has chosen so to behave. But a little reflection will show that most of us, indeed all of us, are to a large extent what we are because we belong to particular societies and to particular groups within those societies. It is obviously not fortuitous that most Arabs are Mohammedans, that most Cinghalese are Buddhists, that most Italians are Roman Catholics, that most Danes are Lutherans. The individual Arabs, Cinghalese, Italians, and Danes have not, with rare exceptions, thought out carefully the meaning of life and weighed the evidence for the truth or falsity of their own and other religions. If you or I had been Arabs or Danes, we should probably have been Mohammedans or Lutherans; it is the fact that we have been born and brought up in England, and not any reasoned and deliberate choice, which make us non-Mohammedan and non-Lutheran. Even within this country the results of local group influence are observable; Methodists are plentiful in Cornwall but scarce in Scotland, whilst the reverse is true of Presbyterians. We do not conclude that most Cornishmen, on careful review of the review of the evidence and arguments, prefer the dogmas and the polity of Methodism, and reject those of Presbyterianism, whilst Scots arrive in large numbers at opposite conclusions. We know perfectly well, when we take the trouble to think, that the majority of Cornishmen or of Scots are Methodists or Presbyterians by virtue of birth rather than by virtue of rational choice.

Or to take another example from the realm of politics. the facts about the War of 1914-1918 have been very differently perceived and interpreted by Britons, Frenchmen, Germans, Italians, and Americans. Germans, with few exceptions, took one view ; Frenchmen, with few exceptions, took another view. Most Britons thought that the war was won mainly by the initial resistance on the Marne and by the pressure of the British Navy. Most Americans would say that American intervention saved the Allies. In Italian schools and in Italian history books the battle of Vittorio Veneto, scarcely known to most Englishmen, is looked upon as the turning point. Quite clearly, though on the subject of that war is to a large extent a group product. Imagine an infant, let us say of neutral birth, adopted by a French family in 1900, or alternatively by a German family, he or she would pretty certainly think and feel differently to-day according to the land of adoption. Yet if he or she were unsophisticated, these thoughts and these feelings would seem to him or to her to result inevitably from the fact or from their consequences.

Helpful Vocabulary :

range in size	تتراوح حجماً ، يتراوح عددها
but for the most part	ولكن في الأغلب
reared by animals	يُرَبَّوْن من قِبَل الحيوانات
solitary confinement	عَزْل انفرادي
damaged by solitude	يتضررون بسبب العُزْلة
defective development	نمو ناقص
human stock	سلالة بشرية
social products	منتوجات اجتماعية ، نتاجات اجتماعية
a little reflection	تفكير قليل ، قليل من التأمُّل
to a large extent	إلى حدّ كبير
we are what we are	نحن ما نحن
truth or falsity	صحة أو بُطلان
if you had been	لو كنتَ ...
reasoned choice	اختيار مُسبَّب
local group influence	تأثير الجماعة المحلية
by virtue of birth	بسبب المولد
rational choice	اختيار عقلاني
American intervention	التدخل الأمريكي
turning point	نقطةُ تحوّلٍ
land of adoption	بلد التبنّي ، أرض التبنّي
with rare exceptions	مع استثناءات نادرة
whilst the reverse	... في حين أنّ العكسّ

Exercise 1 . *Translate the previous passage into Arabic.*

Exercise 2. *Give the Arabic equivalents of these groups of   words :*

1. society   _____ government   _____
    group   _____empire   _____
    community   _____ kingdom   _____
    state   _____ princedom   _____
    country   _____ protectorate _____

2. story   _____ sonnet   _____
    novel   _____ lyric   _____
    drama   _____ ballad   _____
    poem   _____ epic   _____
    verse   _____ novelist   _____
    dramatist   _____ poet   _____

3. sufficient   _____ sufficiency   _____
    efficient   _____ efficiency   _____
    deficient   _____ deficiency   _____

UNIT 30

MOROCCO

The Riff coast.——on the Riff coast Morocco has some hundreds of kilometers along the Mediterranean which was the great highway of ancient civilisation. But this coast which has only open roadsteads has never had a great maritime activity. Furthermore it is hemmed in, almost all the way, by the mountainous barrier of the Jbel and of the Riff. Undoubtedly between Melilla and the Moulouya valley, the plains come down to the sea, but this wide-open gateway only leads to Western Morocco, the steppes leading to the true Morocco.

Doubtless the narrowness of the western end of the Mediterranean has always, encouraged trade between the Riff harbours and the ports of Andalousia : but the Spanish influence resulting from this intercourse was unable to penetrate beyond the little coastal towns in which it sometimes gained ground .

The Coast Jacing Gibraltar.——This coast dominates one of the world's great ocean cross-roads and nowhere else are the shores of Africa and Europe so close to each other. The essential function today of this shore : to command the Passage from the Mediterra-nean to the Atlantic, was as unimportant in the Middle Ages as it was in ancient times. For the Ancients, the Pillars of Hercules marked the end of a world familiar and welcome, the very limits of civilisation .

In the Middle Ages, the Mohammedans rarely ventured into the Atlantic. When in the 16th century the Atlantic and its approaches became primordially important, the Occidental Mohammedans took no part in this development and Practically limited their activities to piracy and so damaged the magnificent trade route which they could have controlled.

For Morocco, this coast was above all a bond with Spain. By this function almost terrestrial, the Straits have over and over again assumed a decisive role in Moroccan history. It was above all to guard the southern flank of Betica that the Romans occupied and kept Northern Morocco. It was the proximity of the two shores Spanish and African which allowed Islam to conquer the Iberian peninsula and which, from the 10th to the 15th century, attached the history of Morocco to that of Mohammedan Spain as regards civilisation.

*The Atlantic coast.*__The Atlantic coast appears to be a long and beautiful maritime façade, on the edge of rich plains leading to the very heart of the country. But no shore is more hostile to maritime life: dead straight and almost shelterless, it is only indented by mediocre harbours and poor estuaries It is above all a breakwater : the great Atlantic swell crashes on to the coastal platform, spreads out in mighty waves which burst into foam on the shore. It has been for centuries Morocco's best rampart.

Thus Morocco has been unlucky with its coasts. Northern Morocco was isolated by its cast and still more by its mountains, the West and the South by the Atlantic.

Helpful Vocabulary :

ancient civilizations	الحضارات القديمة
maritime activity	نشاط بحري
mountainous barrier	حاجز جبلي
come down to	تنحدر إلى
western Morocco	مراكش الغربية ، غرب مراكش
ports of Andalousia	موانئ الأندلس
influence resulting from	التأثير الناشئ من
this intercourse	هذه العلاقة
coastal towns	مدن ساحلية
ocean cross-road	مفترق طرق بحري
essential function	وظيفة رئيسية
the Mediterranean	البحر الأبيض المتوسط
the Atlantic	المحيط الأطلسي
command the passage	يسيطر على المرور
the Middle Ages	العصور الوسطى
Mohammedans	المسلمون
took no part in	لم يشتركوا في
trade route	الطريق التجاري ، طريق التجارة
above all	قبل كل شيء
over and over again	مراراً وتكراراً
decisive role	دور حاسم
Iberian peninsula	شبة جزيرة إيبيريا

Exercise 1 . *Translate the previous passage into Arabic.*

Exercise 2. *Give the Arabic equivalents of these groups of   words :*

1.   shore   _____   island   _____

     beach   _____   peninsula   _____

     coast   _____   isle   _____

     islander   _____   bay   _____

2.   canal   _____   sea   _____

     Channel   _____   lake   _____

     Strait   _____   ocean   _____

     Archipelago   _____   sea route   _____

3.   Greece   _____   Norway   _____

     Ivory Coast   _____   Hague   _____

     The Caspian Sea   _____   Sicily   _____

     Southern Africa   _____   south Africa   _____

     Lesbon   _____   Hungary   _____

     The Jordan   _____   Jordan   _____

UNIT 31

WHY WRITE ?

EACH has his reasons: for one, art is a flight; for another a means of conquering. Bur one can flee into a hermit-age into madness, into age, into madness, into death. One can conquer by arms. Why does one have . Why does it have to be *writing* ? Because, behind the various aims of authors, there is a deeper and more immediate choice which is common to all of us. We shall try to elucidate this choice, and we shall see whether it is not in the name of this very choice of writing that the self-commitment of writers must be required.

Each of our perceptions is accompanied by the con-sciousness that human reality is a 'revealer', that is, it is through human reality that 'there is' being, or to put it differently, that man is the means by which things are mani-fasted. It is our presence in the world which multiplies relations. It is we who set up a relationship between this tree and that bit of sky. Thanks to us, that star which has been dead for millennia, that quarter moon, and that dark river are disclosed in the unity of a landscape. It is the speed of our car and our aeroplane which organizes the great masses of the earth. With each of our acts, the world reveals to us a new face. But, if we know that we are directors of being, we also know that we are not its producers. If we turn away from this landscape, it will sink back into its dark permanence. At least, it will ink back; there is no one mad enough to think that it is going to be annihilated. It is we who shall be annihilated, and the earth will remain in its lethargy until another consciousness comes along to awaken it. Thus, to our inner cerainty of being 'revealers' is added that of being inessential in relation to the thing revealed.

One of the chief motives of artistic creation is certainly

the need of feeling that we are essential in relationship to the world. If I fix on canvas or in writing a certain aspect of the fields or the sea or a look on someone's face which I have disclosed, I am conscious of having produced them by condensing relationships, by introducing order where there was none, by imposing the unity of mind on the diversity of things. That is, I feel myself essential in relation to my creation. But this time it is the created object which escapes me; I cannot reveal and produce at the same time. The creation becomes inessential in relation to the creative activity. First of all, even if it appears finished to others the, the created object always seems to us in a state of suspension; we can always change this line, that shade, that word Thus, it never *forces itself* . A novice painter asked his teacher, 'When should I consider my painting finished?' And the teacher answered, 'When you can look at it in amazement and say to yourself' I'*m* the one who did that'".

Which amounts to saying 'never'. For it is virtually con-sidering one's work with someone else's eyes and revealing what one has created. Bur it is self-evident that we are pro-portionally less conscious of the thing produced and more conscious of our productive activity. When it is a matter of pottery or carpentry, we work according to traditional patterns, with tools whose usage is codified; it is Heidegger's famous ' they ' who are working with our hand, in this case, the result can seem to us sufficiently strange to preserve its objectivity in our eyes. But if we ourselves produce the rules of production, the measures, the criteria, and if our creative drive comes from the very depths of our heart, then we never find anything but ourselves in our work. It is we who have invented the laws by which we judge it. It is our history, our love, our gaiety that we recognize in it. Even if we should look at it without touching it any further, we never *receive* from it that gaiety or love. We put them into it. The results which we have obtained on canvas or paper never seem to us *objective*. We are too familiar with the processes of which they are the effect.

Helpful Vocabulary :

escapes and conquests	الفَرُّ و الكَرُّ
for one	بالنسبة لشخص ما
common to all	مشترك بين الجميع
self-commitment	التزام ذاتي
accompanied by	مصحوبة بـِ
to put it differently	بمعنى آخر
unity of a landscape	وحدة المنظر الطبيعي
dark permanence	ديمومة معتمدة
artistic creation	إبداع فني
condensing relationships	تكثيف العلاقات
introducing order	إدخال النظام
unity and diversity	الوحدة والتعدد
state of suspension	حالة تعليق ، حالة إرجاء
novice painter	رسام مبتدئ
amount to	يصل إلى
with someone else's eyes	بعيون شخص آخر
productive activity	نشاط إبداعي
sufficiently strange	غريب بما فيه الكفاية
creative drive	الدافع الإبداعي
from the depths of our heart	من أعماق القلب
in the name of this very choice	باسم هذا الاختيار ذاته
our presence in the world	وجودنا في العالم

Exercise 1 . *Translate the previous passage into Arabic.*

Exercise 2. *Fill in this table with the suitable English derivatives whenever possible, and write down the Arabic equivalents of all the words.*

Verb		Noun		Adjective	
English	**Arabic**	**English**	**Arabic**	**English**	**Arabic**
		voice			
				deep	
require					
				immediate	
mean					
		moon			
		face			
reveal					
annihilate					
		art			
create					
		hand			
				gay	
preserve					
		amazement			
				united	
				codified	
result					

Exercise 3. *Translate these terms, which are related to the same filed :*

write	_____	columnist	_____
edit	_____	column	_____
editor	_____	article	_____
chief editor	_____	proofread	_____

UNIT 32

LITERATURE

Classical Chinese literature is the literature produced in China during a period of over 3,000 years from the beginning of Chinese history to the Opium War. Its long history and splendid achievements are famous the world over. Its many great writers from all levels of the old society include Qu Yuan, Sima Qian, Tao Yuanming, LiBai, Du Fu, Han Yu, Liu Zongyuan, Su Shi, Li Qingzhao, Xin Qiji, Guan Hanqing, Luo Guanzhong, Shi Naian, Pu Songling and Cao Xueqin. Masterpieces such as the Book of Odes and the "Li Sao", dating from pre-Qin times; Music Bureau ballads and Records of the Historian dating from the Western Han; Tang and Song poetry and lyrics; Yuan drama and Ming and Qing fiction have all greatly enriched the treasure-house of Chinese literature.

(1)   PRE-QIN LITERATURE   (11TH CENTURY B.C.-221 B.C.)

Classical Chinese literature ha its starting point dur-ing the course of the development of Chinese history from slave society to feudal society. The outstanding masterpieces from pre-Qin literature are the Book of Odes dating from the Zhou Dynasty, the historical and philo-sophical prose of the Warring States and the "Li Sao" by Qu Yuan.

The Book of Odes The Book of Odes is the earliest collection of Chinese poetry, and consists of 305 poems written over a period of about 500 years during the West-ern and Spring and Autumn period. It was compiled in the 6th century B.C. and is divided into three parts. The first part, known as "Airs from the States", consists of 160 folk songs from 15 princely states under the Zhou; the "Greater Odes" and "Lesser Odes" make up the second part, consisting of 150 poems; and the "Eulogies", the third part, consists of 40 poems. The divisions are based on musical categories: regional music in the "Airs", music from the area directly under Zhou rule in the "Odes" and religious and ceremonial music in the "Eulogies". The poems in the Book of Odes are actually songs based on these musical types.

In terms of literary value, the fold songs in the "Airs" and "Lesser Odes" are particularly impressive. These oral compositions created by the working people touch on all aspects of current life and society, expressing pro-test at injustice and hope for love and happiness. "Seventh Month" (an air from Bin) describes the year- round arduous toil of the serfs and the oppression under which they suffered; "Cutting Wood" (an air from Wei) chastises the exploiters for enjoying the fruits of labour without working; and "Big Rats" (an air from Wei) ex-presses an even more bitter hatred of the exploiters. "The Broken Axe" and "The Eastern Mountain" (airs from Bin) show the sufferings caused by military campaigns and the people's desire to live inn peace. Songs about love and marriage occupy a considerable portion of the Book of Odes, and most of them are sincere, natural and healthy. The folk songs in the Book of Odes indicate the working people's deep feelings towards life and their profound knowledge of it, in simple, beautiful language and fresh, vivid imagery, fully embodying the artistic creativeness of the people; they are the chief glory of the Book of Odes.

The Book of Odes is China's firs work of realistic literature and as such has had a profound influence on the later development of poetry. Its abundant use of literary devices such as metaphor, allusion, repetition and antiphony has also been highly influential.

Helpful Vocabulary :

classical literature	أدب تقليدي
the Opium War	حرب الأفيون
famous the world over	مشهورة في العالم كله
dating from	يعود تاريخها إلى
slave society	مجتمع العبودية
feudal society	مجتمع الإقطاع ، مجتمع إقطاعي
outstanding masterpieces	روائع عظيمة
historical prose	نثر تأريخي
collection of poetry	مجموعة شعرية
folk songs	أغاني شعبية
regional music	موسيقى محلية
ceremonial music	موسيقى طقوسية ، موسيقى شعائرية
in terms of literary value	من حيث القيمة الأدبية
oral compositions	مُؤَلَّفات شفهية
touch on all aspects of	تَمَسُّ جميع نوحي
protest at injustice	الاحتجاج على الظلم
year-round toil	العناء على مدار العام
fruits of labour	ثمار العمل
hatred of exploiters	كراهية المستغلِّين
military campaigns	حملات عسكرية

Exercise 1 . *Translate the previous passage into Arabic.*

Exercise 2. *Give the Arabic equivalents of these groups of   words :*

1.　　ode　　　　＿＿＿＿＿　　biography　　　＿＿＿＿＿

　　　lyric　　　　＿＿＿＿＿　autobiography　　＿＿＿＿＿

　　　tragedy　　＿＿＿＿＿　comic　　　　　＿＿＿＿＿

　　　comedy　　＿＿＿＿＿　farce　　　　　＿＿＿＿＿

2.　　poetic meter　＿＿＿＿＿　poetic foot　　＿＿＿＿＿

　　　Blank verse　＿＿＿＿＿　rhymed verse　＿＿＿＿＿

3.　　century　　　＿＿＿＿＿　epoch　　　　＿＿＿＿＿

　　　decade　　　＿＿＿＿＿　age　　　　　＿＿＿＿＿

　　　period　　　＿＿＿＿＿　stage　　　　＿＿＿＿＿

UNIT 33
NINETEENTH-CENTURY
ART IN THE UNERED
STATES

Whereas the history of western art had been hitherto almost exclusively linked with European history, its boun-daries extended in the nineteenth century to embrace the art of a young nation which had recently become an independent republic and soon emerged as a world power of considerable political and economic importance — the United States of America. This new republic, unfettered by past traditions and concentrating all its abundant energies on the future, was capable of the highest achieve-ments in every artistic field.

Yet the very absence of tradition, especially in the cultural and artistic fields, was a source of concern to the Americans, who saw it as a vital deficiency. This led them to devote all their enthusiam and admiration to the cultural and artistic inheritance of ancient Europe in all its forms and to try to assimilate it, to make it their own. The tendency was encouraged by the fact that America con-sisted largely of groups of European immigrants who had brought to their new country the customs, the traditions, the fashions, even the artistic styles of their countries of origin.

While a rather passive dependence on European models characterizes the first timid artistic enterprises of the eighteenth century, the nineteenth century in the United States saw a rather freer adaptation of European ideas and, in the field of architecture, the birth of a completely original school. Thus by the end of the century the United States already showed signs of having developed and independent artistic tradition which was in the twentieth century, to prove itself the most mature and the most influential in the world.

In the late eighteenth century, under the influence of French and English models, neo-classicism was already being adopted in north-American architecture with a very high degree of success. This style, which stems from a profound admiration for the ancient Greek and Roman civilizations, is also typical, as in Europe. Of buildings of the first decades of the nineteenth century and clearly reflects the influence of the various American architects who had gathered experience in London, Paris or Rome, while travelling in Europe.

Moreover the adoption of neo-classicism was particularly enthusiastic in the United States, for this new nation cherished the links, sentimental and idealistic, that connected it with the ancient classical civilizations. Both the Roman republic and the Greek city-states were seen as perfect, unsurpassed examples of societies based on those democratic principles which had provided the cornerstone of the American Revolution.

Helpful Vocabulary :

almost exclusively	على وجه الحصر تقريباً
history of western art	تاريخ الفن الغربي
young nation	أمة فَتِيّة
independent republic	جمهورية مستقلة
emerged as a world power	ظهرتْ كقوة عالمية
past traditions	تقاليد الماضي
abundant energies	طاقات وفيرة
artistic field	المجال الفني
source of concern	مصدر قَلَقٍ
vital deficiency	نقص رئيسي
European immigrants	مهاجرون أوروبيون
rather passive dependence	اعتماد سلبي نوعاً ما
freer adaptation	تعديل أكثر حرية
field of architecture	مجال الهندسة المعمارية
original school	مدرسة أصيلة
independent artistic tradition	تقليد فنّي مستقل
profound admiration	إعجاب عميق
Greek city-states	الدول المدن اليونانية
unsurpassed examples	أمثلة رائعة
democratic principles	مبادئ ديمقراطية

Exercise 1 . *Translate the previous passage into Arabic.*

Exercise 2. *Fill in this table with the suitable English   derivatives whenever   possible, and write down   the Arabic equivalents of all the   words.*

Verb		Noun		Adjective	
English	Arabic	English	Arabic	English	Arabic
		art			
embrace					
				exclusive	
		republic			
emerge					
encourage					
		deficiency			
				free	
devote					
		concern			
				fashionable	
		adaptation			
				democratic	
develop					
		influence			
				perfect	
connect					
		classicism			

Exercise 3. *Translate these pairs :*

extend	_____	extent	_____
devise	_____	device	_____
advise	_____	advice	_____
past	_____	passed	_____
deficiency	_____	efficiency	_____

UNIT 34

THE LARYNX AND
VOICING

The **larynx** is a very important vocal organ which contains two very tiny muscles down in the throat that can create a sound _ though a very faint, weak sound _ by vibrating. Though it is a tin organ, all speech is described with reference to what the larynx is doing. The larynx itself or the muscles inside it are called by several different terms. Including **voice box, vocal bands. vocal folds** and **vocal cords**. The vocal cords are housed inside the protective cartilage familiarly known as the "Adam's Apple".

You can see in the alternate names for the muscles of the larynx the analogy to rubber bands or to the cords of a musical instrument Raising the pitch of the voice involves tightening the muscles of the larynx. and lowering the pitch of the voice means loosening them. If you loosen them too much. You will actually lose voice completely, as the cords are too slack to sustain vibration.

The larynx is completely closed when swallowing. When breathing normally or resting. It is slack and open. So that air can go in and out of the space between the muscles. The space, or opening, between the muscles is called the glottis. The shape and size of the glottis has a dra-matic effect on the sound which is produced and ultimately heard as speech. An oval-shaped elastic band is a good visual model of the vocal cords. With the hole in the middle representing the glottis.

For some segmental speech sounds, the larynx is open and air just passes through the slack vocal cords. The air is later modified in the mouth to make a particular sound. An example is the consonant]p[, as in *put* or *supper*. This consonant is nothing but air (the **breath stream** from the lungs) which has been modified by (1) closing the lips, (2) let-ting the air pressure build up a little behind the closed lips and then (3) expelling the air.

The type of sound represented by]p[. which involves only modi-fication of the shape of the column of air coming up through the open glottis. is called **voiceless**. Another example of a voiceless consonant is]f [, like]p[,]f[is nothing but a breath of stream with a certain modification of that column of air in the mouth. This time the modification involves not the two lips, but rather the top teeth and the bot-tom lip

For another major class of speech sounds, the vocal folds are brought close together and tightened, narrowing the glottis. When air passes through the narrowed glottis. the vocal folds vibrate and make a sound, called a **vocal buzz**. This is a very faint sound caused by the vibrating vocal cords. This basic vocal buzz is later amplified in the **resonance chamber** __ of the mouth (the **oral chamber**) and/or the nose (the nasal chamber). Speech sounds produced with vibrating vocal cords are referred to as **voiced**.

An example of a voiced consonant is]b[. like]p[,]b[is produced by bringing the two lips together and then releasing the air built up behind that closure. Unlike]p[, however, the vocal folds are vibrating during the production of]v [differs from]f[only in the fact that]f[is produced without vocal fold vibration, while]v[requires vocal fold vibration for its production. If you put hands over your ears or touch your Adam's Apple as you alternate prolonged productions of]f[and]v[, you should be able to hear and feel the vocal cords turning on and off their vibration (Ladefoged 1982: 2) you can also hear the difference between voiced and voiceless sounds very clearly by pro-ducing a sustained vowel sound such as]aaaa[and then pronouncing the same vowel in a whispered manner. The normal vowel is voiced; the whispered vowel is voiceless. When not whispered, all vowels in English (and most languages) are voiced. Consonants may be either voiced or voiceless.

For both voiced and voiceless sounds, the nature of the basic sound at the glottis__ either the buzz or the naked puff of air coming up from the lungs __ is modified in the oral chamber, with or without coupling to the nasal chamber. There are many, many possible modification, as will be introduced in the next three chapters.

Phonetics and phonology.

Phonology is the study and description of the patterning of the noises and silences of speech in regular ways within particular languages.

Phonetics is the study and description of the nature of the raw noises and silences of speech. Phonetics is thus the basis for phonology, and phonology can be said to build on phonetics and to be a more general and abstract pursuit than phonetics.

We language teachers are primarily interested in phonology, that is, in the patterns of sounds which make up speech. However, we must also concern ourselves with phonetics, which is the basis for phon-ology. If the characteristics of individual speech sounds are carefully investigated and precisely described phonetically, then we well be on a firm basis for investigating and describing how the individual sounds pattern within a given language.

Helpful Vocabulary :

larynx	الحنجرة
vocal organ	عضو صوتي
voice box	صندوق الصوت
vocal cords	الحبال الصوتية
Adam's apple	تفاحة آدم
pitch of the voice	نغمة الصوت
glottis	المِزمَار
dramatic effect	تأثير كبير
segmental speech sounds	أصوات الكلام القِطعِيَّة
breath stream	تَيَّار النَّفَس
consonants and vowels	الصوامت والصوائت
voiceless sound	صوت مهموس
voiced sound	صوت مجهور
resonance chamber	تجويف الرنين
oral chamber	تجويف فموي
nasal chamber	تجويف أنفي
vocal fold vibration	اهتزاز الحبال الصوتية
whispered vowel	صائت مُوَشْوَش
housed inside	محفوظةٌ في
tightening and loosening	شدّ وإرخاء
voiced consonant	صامت مجهور

Exercise 1 . *Translate the previous passage into Arabic.*

Exercise 2. *Give the Arabic equivalents of these groups of   words :*

1. stop   _____   semi-vowel   _____

    affricate   _____   nasal   _____

    fricative   _____   glide   _____

2. labial   _____interdental   _____

    bilabial   _____alveolar   _____

    dental   _____lingual   _____

    velar   _____velum   _____

    nasal   _____velarize   _____

    nasalize   _____   apex   _____

    nasalization   _____   vocal cords   _____

    lateral   _____   bilateral   _____

3. high vowel   _____   front vowel   _____

    central vowel   _____   mid vowel   _____

    low vowel   _____   back vowel   _____

    rounded vowel   _____   devoiced vowel   _____

UNIT 35

PRONUNCIATION AND SPELING

It is not really understood how the spoken language operates ▬ whether as the output of a servo-mechanism ▬ that is, a complex system with feedback loops monitoring itself and modifying itself as it hoes along ▬ or by something else equally complex . To most speakers it simply doesn't matter how it operates so long as it does One can but marvel that millions of people can communicate daily by speech and manage their linguistic relationships with no more than relatively unimportant misunderstandings.

It is all the more mysterious how it comes about that if one moves just a few miles away from one's own habitat a different set of lin-guistic sounds is encountered ▬ still those of recognizably the same language but subtly and charmingly different ▬ and that one does not even need to move outside one's immediate area to encounter other observably different set of sounds representing social or educational rather than geographical distancings form oneself.

These general considerations are true of all languages which in historical time have remained geographically static. Variation is governed by the social arrangements within a group or clan. or by a geographical boundary like a river or a line of mountains. And within the borders and limits of a given set of a given set of variants of one language it is quite normal to find other people using totally unintelligible sets of sounds (foreign languages like Welsh) or half-way houses (one's own language spoken by foreigners).

Over the centuries the movement of clans and tribes of people has produced the kind of crop that would emerge if a blind god had sprinkled seeds at random on a field ▬ a vast array of diverse patterns, usually not even interlocking or decussated, but crossed and intersected by every kind of structured diversity.

Of all the main languages of the world none is more widely dissemiated and more subtly sliced and severed than English. and all within the space of only 1,500 years. From the diversity of the were already divided into a multitude of linguistic subgroups using different modes of pronunciation, grammar, and usage.

even though they remained (as far as we can tell) mutually intel-ligible.

I regard it as axiomatic that the traditional classification of Anglo-Saxon, dialect into four major groups — Northumbrian. Mercian, West Saxon, and Kentish — is an over-simplification. If more information about them had survived, the parental group-ings of the numerous varieties of English now spoken in Britain would have been more than quadrilaterally complex. Even now, if all recorded forms of every surviving text were fed into a computer databank in an unregularized form, and without prior assumptions, new distributional maps would emerge, and the overlaid rules of the main types of *Schriftsprache* could perhaps be stripped away to take us nearer to the tribal variations of speech extant at the time of Offa, Alfred , and Elfric. Regional variation of speech at the time of the first discernibly professional analyses of dialects — in practice not before the seventeenth century — points firmly in the direction of great complexity. It seems most unlikely that this complexity developed from a simple base of four 'blocks' of Anglo-Saxon speech.

Be that as it may, we must work with the evidence we have. The establishment of the mode of pronunciation of the earliest form of English is traditionally and necessarily based on an assumption of close equivalence between sound and symbol. Phonologists assume near-coincidence between spellings and sounds in the earliest records of our language: that OE. *hus* 'house' is /hu:s/; OE. hlud 'loud' is /hlu:d/, with initial *h* fully pronounced and with a long u; *hring* 'ring' is /hrin/, also with *h* fully pronounced but with n not ng; and that OE. *wlanc is/ wlank/* , with the approximant *w* fully pronounce before the following/ . in may view it is likely that some Anglo-Saxon tribes, or groups of people within tribes, had already adopted the later ways of pronouncing such words.

Traditional phonology is based on the assumption that three major phonetic changes at a later period brought radical changes to the classes of words into which these four words fall — that /hu:s/ became / haus/as part of the Great Vowel Shift; that *h* followed by the liquid consonants/ and *r* was lost at the beginning of the Middle English period; and that words beginning with *wl* (an approximant followed by the liquid consonant) disappeared in the course of the Middle English period. We should, however, allow for the possibility that dissident pronunciations existed among minority groups within the Anglo-Saxon period, and that the historical process was one in which these 'subversive' forms gradually replaced the ones maintained by the conservative scribes in their written texts and by linguistic conservatives in their speech.

Helpful Vocabulary :

spoken language	اللغة المَحْكية
complex system	نظام معقد
feedback loops	دوائر التغذية الراجعة
immediate area	المنطقة المباشرة
sets of sounds	مجموعات من الأصوات
general considerations	اعتبارات عامة
crossed and intersected	متصالب ومتقاطع
structured diversity	تنوع مركَّب
more widely disseminated	أوسع انتشاراً
within the space of	ضمن مدى ، ضمن فترة
modes of pronunciation	أنماط من النطق
traditional classification	تصنيف تقليدي
computer databank	بنك بيانات مُحَوْسَب
in an unregularized from	بشكل غير منتظم
without prior assumptions	دون افتراضات سابقة
distributional maps	خرائط توزيع
tribal variations	تنوُّعات قَبَلِيَّة
in practice not before	عملياً ليس قَبَلِيَّة
most unlikely	غير محتمل جداً
be that as it may	ومهما يكنْ من أمر
close equivalence	تكافؤ متقارب
sound and symbol	الصوت والرمز

Exercise 1 . *Translate the previous passage into Arabic.*

Exercise 2. *Fill in this table with the suitable English derivatives whenever possible, and write down the Arabic equivalents of all the words.*

Verb		Noun		Adjective	
English	Arabic	English	Arabic	English	Arabic
vary					
		grammar			
				complex	
emerge					
		tribe			
				relative	
cross					
intersect					
		analysis			
				recognizable	
				intelligible	
encounter					
		border			
				true	
slice					
		evidence			
				regional	
severe					

Exercise 3. *Translate these linguistic terms :*

hissing sound   _____   initial phoneme   _____

silent letter   _____   dialect   _____

medial phoneme   _____   idiolect   _____

final phoneme   _____   jargon   _____

UNIT 36

THE PSYCHOLOGY OF
AESTHETICS

TH E R E can be few topics more certain to lead to furious discussion than those related to aesthetics; there can be few topics within the realm of aesthetics more certain to arouse normally peaceful artists, philosophers, and aestheticians to a pitch of uncontrolled indignation than that which has given this chapter its title. The idea that objects of beauty as well as their creation and appreciation, are subject to scientific scrutiny appears abhorrent to most people, even as the idea that the physicist might study and analyse the colours of the rainbow with his objective methods was ab-horrent to their grandparents. There appears to exist a fear that clumsy handing might crush the butterfly's wings; an idea that analysis may destroy what it is intending to study.

Associated with this fear is perhaps another. Most people hold views regarding aesthetics which they are extremely unwilling to give up, although these views are not based on any objective facts. Indeed, the very idea that one's views ought to be related to factual evidence is usually dismissed, and it is asserted that subjectivity reigns supreme in this field. This, of course, is a tenable view; it contradicted, however, by the well-known tendency of most people to argue about their aesthetic views, often with great acerbity, always with great tenacity, never with that humility which the hypothesis of complete subjectivity should engender in them. If aesthetic judgements are completely subjective, there would appear as little point in argument as in scien-tific experiment; if the one is permissible, so surely is the other. Perhaps the objection to scientific investigation is in part due to a fear that facts may be more potent than argu-ments in forcing one to give up a cherished position, and to

Acknowledge certain objective factors which one would pre-fer to overlook.

However that may be, there can be little doubt about the hostile reaction which psychology has experienced on all sides when it attempted to introduce scientific methods into the study of aesthetics. A good deal of this hostility is prob-ably based on misunderstanding, and it will be the purpose of this chapter to explain in some detail just what the psycho-logist is trying to do, and how he sets about his task. I shall try to avoid arguments and comparisons with philosophical procedures and problems as far as possible; these often seem to resemble those attacked by psychologists, but the simi-larity is only superficial. The reader familiar with modern aesthetic doctrines, and with the long history of discussions in this field, will easily be able to apply the facts of psycho-logical research to the solution of such philosophical prob-lems as interest him.

How, then, does the psychologist start? He notices that certain types of judgement are made frequently of certain objects; these judgements are phrased in items of 'beautiful' and 'ugly', or some synonymous terms, and apply to various combinations of colours and shapes, as in the visual arts; words, as in poetry ; or sounds, as in music. The essential datum with which he deals, therefore , is a relation— a rela-tion between a stimulus (picture, poem, piece of music) and a person who reacts to this stimulus in certain conventional ways. Usually the response is a verbal one, but it is possible, and has been found useful in certain situations, to record physiological reactions indicative of emotion, such as heart-beat, pulse-rate, skin temperature, or changes in the electric conductivity of the skin.

In analyzing this relation, the psychologist encounters a twofold problem. In the first place, he must ask himself : Just what is the physical property of the stimulus which causes a favourable reaction as opposed to an unfavour-able reaction in the majority of the subjects with whom he is working? In the second place, he must ask himself : Just what is the reason why one person reacts favour-ably to a given stimulus, while another person reacts un-favourably ?

Helpful Vocabulary :

psychology of aesthetics	علم نفس الجمال
furious discussion	جدال صاخب
uncontrolled indignation	غضب خارج عن السيطرة
subject to	خاضع لِ
objective methods	أساليب موضوعية
associated with	مُقْتَرِنٌ بِـ
views regarding	آراء تتعلق بِـ
the very idea	الفكرةُ ذاتُها
subjectivity reigns supreme	الذاتية لها السَّبْقُ
well-known tendency	مَيْل معروف
with humility	بتواضع
scientific investigation	استقصاء علمي
is in part due to	جزئياً يُعْزَى إلى
however that may be	ومهما يكنْ من أمر
hostile reaction	رَدُّ فِعْلٍ مُعَادٍ
based on misunderstanding	قائم على سوء الفهم
in some detail	بشيء من التفصيل
as far as possible	بقدر الإمكان
superficial similarity	تشابه سطحي
synonymous terms	مصطلحات مرادِفة
visual arts	الفنون المرئية
conventional ways	طرق تقليدية

Exercise 1 . *Translate the previous passage into Arabic.*

Exercise 2. *Choose the suitable prepositions* :

1. This theory leads (to, far) certain applications.

2. What he did will be subject (in, to) questioning .

3. An increase in pluse-rate is usually associated (with, by) fear

4. His views are based (on, at) facts .

5. Her opinions are contradicted (with, by) his opinions .

6. They object (to, on) what he suggests .

7. Diseases are sometimes due (by, to) poverty .

8. They attempt to introduce computers (in, into) modern   education .

9. Can you phrase it (in, with) other words ?

10. what is the reason (of, for) such problems ?

UNIT 37

YOUR KEY TO A
BERRER LIFE

The most important psychologic discovery of this cen-tury is the discovery of the "self-image." Whether we real-ize it or not, each of us carries about with us a mental blueprint or picture of ourselves. It may be vague and ill-defined to our conscious gaze. In fact, it may not be consciously recognizable at all. But it is there. complete down to the last detail. This self-images is our own con-ception of the "sort of person I am. " It has been built up from our own *beliefs* about ourselves. But most of these beliefs about ourselves have unconsciously been formed from our past experiences, our successes and failures, our humiliation, our triumphs, and the way other people have reacted to us, especially in early childhood. From all these we mentally construct a "self" (or a picture of a self). Once an idea or belief about ourselves goes into this pic-ture it becomes "true," as far as we personally are con-cerned. We do not question its validity, but proceed to act upon it *just as if it were true*.

This self-image becomes a golden key to living a better life because of two important discoveries :

(1) All your actions, feelings, behavior ___ even your abilities___ even your abilities___ are always consistent with this self-image.

In short, you will "act like" the sort of person you con-ceive yourself to be. Not only this, but you literally can-not act otherwise, in spite of all your conscious efforts or will power. The man who conceives himself to be "fail-ure-type person' will find some way to fail, in spite of all his good intentions, or his will power, even if opportunity is literally dumped in his lap. The person who conceives himself to be a victim of injustice, on "who was meant

To suffer," will invariably find circumstances to verify his opinions.

The self-images is a "premise," a base, or a foundation upon which your entire personality, your behavior, and even your circumstances are built. Because of this our ex-periences seem to verify, and thereby strengthen our self images, and a vicious or a beneficent cycle, as the case may be, is set up.

For example, a schoolboy who sees himself as an "F" type student, or one who is "dumb in mathematics," will invariably find that his report card bears him out . He then has "proof." A young girl who has and image of herself as the sort of person nobody likes will find indeed that she is avoided at the school dance. She literally invites re-jection. Her woe-begone expression, her hang-dog man-ner, her over-anxiousness to please, or perhaps her un-conscious hostility towards those she anticipates will affront her—all act to drive away those whom she would attract. In the same manner, a salesman or a businessman will also find that his actual experiences tend to "prove" his self-image is correct.

Because of this objective "proof" it very seldom occurs to a person that his trouble lies in his self-image or his own evaluation of himself . Tell the schoolboy that he only "thinks" he cannot master algebra, and he will doubt your sanity. He has tried and tried, and still his report cart tells the story. Tell the salesman that it is only and idea that he cannot earn more than a certain figure, and he can prove you wrong by his order book. He knows only too well how hard he has tried and failed. Yet, as we shall see later, almost miraculous changes have occurred both in grades of students, and in the earning capacity of sales-men—when they were prevailed upon to change their self-images.

(2) The self-image can be changed. Numerous case his-tories have shown that one is never too young not too old to changes his self-image and thereby start to live a new life.

Helpful Vocabulary :

self-image	صورة ذاتية ، صورة عن الذات
pyshological discovery	اكتشاف نفسي
whether we realize it or not	سواء أعرفنا ذلك أم لم نعرف
conscious gaze	نظرة واعية
mental picture	صورة ذهنية
consciously recognizable	معروفة بوعي
to the last detail	حتى آخر تفصيلاتها
to act upon it	يعمل بموجبها
vicious cycle	دائرة مفرغة
" F " student	طالب راسب
dumb in mathematics	جاهل في الرياضيات
invite rejection	تدعو إلى الرفض
over-anxiousness	تَلَهُّف زائد
unconscious hostility	عداء لا شعوري
salesman	موظَّف مبيعات
very seldom occur	يحدث نادراً جداً
his trouble lies in	تكمن المشكلة في
his evaluation of himself	تقييمه لنفسه
report card	بطاقة التقرير
order book	دفتر طالبات الشراء
case history	تاريخ الحالة
doubt his sanity	يشك في سلامة عقله

Exercise 1 . *Translate the previous passage into Arabic.*

Exercise 2. *Fill in this table with the suitable English derivatives whenever possible, and write down the Arabic equivalents of all the words.*

Verb		Noun		Adjective	
English	Arabic	English	Arabic	English	Arabic
		discovery			
				mental	
				vague	
		conception			
				conscious	
		failure			
				complete	
		triumph			
construct					
		humiliation			
				true	
		experience			
				literal	
invite					
		evaluation			
				miraculous	
occur					
grade					

Exercise 3. *Translate these words, giving two meanings of each :*

doubt	_____	_____	experience	_____	_____
picture	_____	_____	report	_____	_____
gaze	_____	_____	dance	_____	_____
complete	_____	_____	form	_____	_____

UNIT 38

THE SCIENTIFIC
METHOD

The essence of academic life is dispute. Mediaeval scholars debated how many angels could sit upon the head of a pin, a matter that has still not been finally resolved. This great tradition lives on and thus a clear statement of a position is the life blood of the academic world. It will be seized upon with as much avidity as intellectual torpor allows (all things are relative) and fine exhi-bitions of hair splitting, references to authorities, footnotes to footnotes will be made. In the Germanic tradition of scholarship the longest list of references will win the day. This makes it exceedingly difficult to state with any precision or clarity what constitutes the scientific method.

Nevertheless scientists do carry out experiments. They use their findings to develop theories and put them to the test with further experiment. Thus despite the problems of defining scientific method, there are *de facto* definitions in daily use in laboratories throughout the world. Philosophers of science, many of whom have never conducted an experiment in their lives, might well throw up their hands in horror at such a definition, but scientific method can be seen as essentially what scientists do. This is the working definition which I shall adopt in this chapter and to ensure its relevance to our aims and purposes, I will restrict myself to the methods used in psychology.

The scientific method

Nevertheless, given the problems of defining the scientific method and the not inconsiderable philosophical literature on its nature, I shall briefly examine some of the difficulties in this area, in order that may somewhat pragmatic, not to say behavioural, approach in defining the method, can be free of philosophic error.

Many working scientists, I think it is fair to say, follow the scientific logic of their work advocated by Karl Popper in *The logic of scientific Discovery*. The essence of this approach, to risk a gross simplification, is that in science, hypotheses must be expressed in a refutable form. Science is then concerned with the refutation of hypothese. All scientific knowledge is thus provisional. At any point it may be refuted. There is no doubt that, in psychology at least, a large number of experiments are carried out on this principle. Nevertheless the study of the history of science reveals that in many cases great discoveries and theories were not thus made. As Chalmers has pointed out (1978), Newton's gravitational theory appeared to be refuted by observations of the movements of the moon. However it was not in fact rejected. In addition there is the philosophical difficulty that observations which are supposed to falsify theories or hypotheses are themselves theory dependent. Chalmers again supplies a nice astronomical example from the work of Copernicus whose theory implied that Venus should appear to change size during the year. Naked eye observation appeared to refute the claim. However, such naked eye observation has a theoretical supposition that the eye can estimate the size of small light sources. In fact, this theory assumption is wrong, as telescopic observation demonstrates. Finally, there is a further objection to the simple falsification approach – namely that, in fact, as the history of science demonstrates scientist are often happy to have their hypotheses confirmed.

This last point is important because even if a simple experiment is designed to put a hypothesis to the empirical test and the hypothesis is not rejected, most workers would regard that hypothesis as supported albeit tentatively. This is certainly the case in many psychological experiments. Here, however, an important distinction is drawn by philosophers of science. If a theory yields new and surprising hypotheses, especially when contra-intuitive, then confirmation is considered good support for theory. This is confirmation of bold conjectures. On the other hand, cautious conjectures that follow easily from the theory are only interesting if falsified. Now it is my contention that in psychology this approach has been grossly abused. Psychologists rarely go in for bold conjectures. Rather they use cautious conjec-tures and regard the theory as confirmed if they are supported. This is particularly true of the users of cognitive models described in the next chapter.

Because of these problems with the notion of refutability, even if the confirmation of novel hypotheses is allowed, some philos-ophers of science have argued that the scientific method is far more complex, involving whole programmes of work as discussed by Lakatos and (what has become very popular and current jargon in psychology) paradigms, as discussed by Kuhn (1975) .

Helpful Vocabulary :

academic life	الحياة الأكاديمية ، الحياة العلمية
mediaeval scholars	علماء القرون الوسطى
life blood	دم الحياة
exceedingly difficult	صعب جداً
with any precision	بأية دِقّة
carry out experiments	يقومون بالتجارب
put them to the test	يُخْضعونها للفحص ، يفحصونها
de facto definitions	تعريفات الأمر الواقع
in horror at	فَزَعاً مِنْ
restrict myself to	أحْصُر نفسي في
in order that	من أجَل أنَّ
free of error	خالصة من الخطأ
scientific logic	المنطق العلمي
essence of this approach	جوهر هذا النهج
refutation of hypotheses	رفض الفرضيات
provisional knowledge	معرفة مؤقتة
gravitational theory	نظرية الجاذبية
falsify theories	يدحض النظريات
theory dependent	معتمد على نظرية
astronomical example	مَثَلّ فلكي
naked eye observation	الملاحظة بالعين المجردة
telescopic observation	ملاحظة مِقْرابِيّة ، ملاحظة بالمِقْراب

Exercise 1 . *Translate the previous passage into Arabic.*

Exercise 2. *Fill in this table with the suitable English derivatives whenever possible, and write down the Arabic equivalents of all the words.*

Verb		Noun		Adjective	
English	**Arabic**	**English**	**Arabic**	**English**	**Arabic**
		essence			
resolve					
		dispute			
		blood			
conduct					
		exhibition			
restrict					
				tentative	
		simplification			
				empirical	
falsify					
		distinction			
confirm					

Exercise 3. *Translate these terms :*

physiological psychology

social psychology   _____

psychometry   _____

psychomotor   _____

psychomotor skill   _____

psychomotor test   _____

puberty   _____

public health   _____

public examination   _____

public library   _____

UNIT 39

KNOWLEDGE AND
MASTERY OF
LANGUAGE

It is in the nature of language to impose system and order, to offer us sets of choices from which we must choose one way or another of building our inner world. Without that order we should never be able to start building, but there is always the danger of over-acceptance. How many teachers, even today, welcome and enjoy the power of young people to coin new words to set alongside the old order? How often do social pressures prevent us exercising our power to modify the meaning of words by improvising a new context, as in metaphor? Sometimes, it seems, our pupils are more aware than we are of the fact that language is living and changing; we could help them more often to explore and test out its mew possibilities. Inevitably, thought, the weight of our experience lies in a mature awareness of the possibilities and limitations raised by the more permanent forms of order in language. There has already been an explicit case (at our own level) in this chapter. The question "what is English?" invites a different form of answer from, say, "what at our best are we doing in English classes?"if we wish to describe a process, *composition* for example the first question will tend to suggest the finished product (the marks on the page even) rather than the activity of bringing together and composing the disorder of our experience. "What … doing" will suggest nominal forms of verbs (bringing, composing) and thus help to keep activities in mind.

At a much simpler level members of the Seminar noted that some of us referred to "talk to "talk" in class, others to "speech". In order to see why one might consider some of the contexts in which the words are used. "Talk" tends to be used of less formal occasions___ "give a speech/ give a talk". In some contexts "speech" implies accent or pronunciation___ "good speech, classroom speech"; "classroom talk" may then be used as the generic term, even though in normal con-texts we use "spoken and written, speech and writing" and not "talk" .

"Speech" seems to be rarely used today for verbal interaction, whereas we do say "we talked about it, talked it over, had a heart to heart talk". Tentatively, one might assume that those who preferred "talk" wanted to encourage informal interaction interaction in class; those who preferred "speech" were perhaps hoping for sustained and organized utterance (rather than "chat"). Unit difference like this are made explicit one may be trapped in a general uneasiness about what the other man means. Equally, in making the difference explicit we may begin to look more acutely at what goes on in class.

There is, then, a kind of knowledge or awareness about language that affects our power to think clearly and "to some purpose", in Susan Stebbing's words. Whatever the subject in the curriculum, the places where such knowledge can affect language in operation need to be more fully understood than they are at present. But the teacher of English will be particularly concerned with helping pupils, in the terms of one report, to "conceptualize their awareness of language". This seemingly cumbersome phrase was chosen with some care. "Conceptualizing", a verbal form, suggests *activity* on the part of the individual pupil, whereas "concepts" unfortunately can be thought of as things, reified objects to be handed over by the teacher. "Their awareness" points to a recognition already there in the pupil's thinking, not yet explicit or fully conscious perhaps, but something the alert teacher will notice and draw on.

The notion of gaining a new control over what we think by increase-ing our conceptual awareness of language in general has an obvious appeal to a gathering of intellectuals, not least when many of them are linguists! However, the final repots were cautious in their claims for such knowledge at the school stage. The first question at issue is when and how the knowledge becomes explicit. There was some agreement that the answer should apply to an individual rather than an age group. For if we teachers encourage a pupil to conceptualize, we should ideally be doing this at the point where the demands at the operational level of language have already given our pupil the sense that conceptualizing is needed. As experienced teachers we should see this demand emerging and be ready to help it on the way. In other words, our knowledge of the route ahead is not something to impose on the student—— thus robbing him of the delight of discovery and maybe dissociating such discoveries as he does make from the systematic framework he "received" from us.

Helpful Vocabulary :

nature of language	طبيعة اللغة
sets of choices	مجموعات من الاختيارات
to coin new words	ليكوّنوا كلمات جديدة
how often ?	كم مرةً
social pressures	ضغوطات اجتماعية
mature awareness	إدراك مُتَأَنٍّ ، إدراك مدروس
explicit case	حالة ظاهرة
members of the Seminar	أعضاء الندوة
less formal occasions	مناسبات أقل رسمية
normal contexts	سياقات عادية
verbal interaction	تفاعل لفظي
it some purpose	لهدفٍ ما
language in operation	اللغة في الاستعمال
in the terms of one report	وِفْقًا لأحد التقارير
alert teacher	المعلّم اليَقِظ
obvious appeal	إغراء واضح
a gathering of intellectuals	مجموعة من المفكرين ، مجموعة من رجال الفكر
the question at issue	القضيّة الجَدَلية ، القضيّة المثيرة للجَدَل
age group	فِئَة عُمْرية
experienced teachers	معلمون ذو خبرة
delight of discovery	متعة الاكتشاف

170

Exercise 1 . *Translate the previous passage into Arabic.*

Exercise 2. *Fill in this table with the suitable English derivatives whenever possible, and write down the Arabic equivalents of all the words.*

Verb		Noun		Adjective	
English	**Arabic**	**English**	**Arabic**	**English**	**Arabic**
offer					
choose					
		danger			
accept					
		fact			
				normal	
change					
				verbal	
enjoy					
		exercise			
				generic	
		activity			
modify					
		heart			
				formal	
order					
		context			
				organized	

Exercise 3. *Translate these educational terms :*

ABC method	الطريقة الهجائية	case method	_____
analytical method	_____	combined method	_____
anecdotal method		comparative method	
audio-lingual method	_____	cumulative method	_____
audio-visual method	_____	deductive method	
mimicry method	_____	inductive method	_____

171

UNIT 40

WHAT IS GOOD TEACHING ?

At a meeting concerned with planning the curriculum of a new uni-versity, the University of south Florida. I asked a distinguished visiting professor from the University of Chicago the attributes of a good teacher. He replied that there are only two essentials : to be "an interesting per-son " and to be "well educated." Few could argue with these two attri-butes, but they are so general that they do not go much beyond Mammy Yokum's framed motto hanging over her mantelpiece which announces that "Good is better than evil because it is nicer."

The real problem concerns the particulars as to what is meant by "an interesting person" and "well-educated." From the tone of his answer I surmised that the Chicago professor would agree with Robert Hutchins about the lack of importance of methodology. (He was, in fact, a great admirer of Hutchins.) Nevertheless. I can certainly agree with both of his essentials as far as they go. Yet the first requisite of a good teacher__ that he not be boring__ must be qualified as to techniques used to ac-complish this end. Some highly paid comedians are interesting persons to their audiences but the philosophy, psychology, and sociology, which some of them practice are not the procedures of the good teacher. Also a teacher can be interesting in a classroom by depending on cheap efforts off-color stories, picking on awkward members of the class , or just being a smart aleck in general. Yet the need for such techniques is proof that he is a poor rather than a good teacher. A good teacher does not "jazz up" his presentations so that the jazz either outshines or coun-teracts the central theme of the subject he is supposed to be teaching. The best teacher may have a fine sense of humor, but he keeps interest alive through his knowledge of his students and the world. Such knowl-edge enables the teacher to generate excitement by dwelling on the spirit and quality of intellectual experiences. We all need to remember, as Clifton Fadiman has said, "School is still the main, sometimes the only chart to the most glamorous of all Treasure Islands ___ the child's own mind."

Being an "interesting person" and a "well-educated person" are parts of the same fabric and must be especially so for the teacher. Although each is a part of the other, neither knowledge of process nor knowledge of subject matter alone makes the good teacher. But both of these requisites were combined in the "1961" Teacher of the year" of whom her principal remarked: "She gives her students the kind of salt that makes them thirsty for knowledge." A teacher can create such a desire to learn only when process and subject matter are well interrelated. Education then becomes an exciting adventure of learning what is relevant. The soundest method cannot make innocuous subject matter interesting to intelligent people. But a synthesis of sound method and sound subject-matter can provide the kind " of salt that makes them thirsty for know[-edge."

Teaching what is relevant is teaching what is concerned with the world of today. This does not mean, however, that yesterday and tomorrow are forgotten. It only means that if one does not live for today one does not live at all because, obviously, yesterday is gone and tomorrow is not here. Yet the good teacher does use the learning of both yesterday and today in preparing his students for tomorrow. For instance, in teaching what is relevant to the world of today he needs to maintain the spirit of the Platonic tradition in which truth, beauty, and goodness are para-mount.

One can be interesting even in using the lecture technique of teaching alone if he can utilize brevity, point (or relevance), and wit. I have elaborated on relevance and wit but brevity is also important if the student preparing t become a teacher is to be an interesting talker. And incidentally, talking and teaching are not necessarily synonymous. Teach-ing candidates might remember that the greatest ministers of the churches of our nation spend almost a whole week preparing for one sermon or lecture, and most of them are careful not to take more than twenty minutes to deliver it. This emphasizes not only the importance of brevity in speech but also the need for much study.

Probably the surest and best way for a teacher to make a class inter-esting is simply to get the students so involved in their own educational process that they put so much intelligence and vigor in their work that it becomes a part of them. The question, then, is how to get them so involved? We will try to answer it briefly by saying that the subject the students are studying must be clearly shown as having personal impor-tance to them and the teacher must make possible for them some real experiences which are of significance.

Helpful Vocabulary :

planning the curriculum	تخطيط المنهج
visiting professor	أستاذ زائر
framed motto	شعار مُؤطَّر ، شعار في إطار
central theme	الموضوع الرئيسي
tone of his answer	نغمة جوابه
sense of humor	روح الدُّعابة
not be boring	ألا يكون مُمِلاًّ
cheap efforts	محاولات رخيصة
intellectual experiences	خبرات عقلية
thirsty for knowledge	متعطِّش للمعرفة
desire to learn	الرغبة في التعلُّم
exciting adventure	مغامرة مثيرة
Platonic tradition	التقليد الأفلاطوني
lecture technique	أسلوب المحاضرة
not necessarily synonymous	ليسا بالضرورة مترادفين
importance of brevity	أهمية الاختصار
intelligence and vigor	ذكاء ونشاط
of significance	ذو أهمية
dictionary definition	تعريف مُعْجميّ

Exercise 1 . *Translate the previous passage into Arabic.*

Exercise 2. *Fill in this table with the suitable English derivatives whenever possible, and write down the Arabic equivalents of all the words.*

Verb		Noun		Adjective	
English	**Arabic**	**English**	**Arabic**	**English**	**Arabic**
announce					
		curriculum			
				distinguished	
concern					
		professor			
bore					
		requisite			
				synthetic	
		quality			
		relevance			
				brief	
present					
		emphasis			
				careful	
excite					
		significance			
				involved	
elaborate					

Exercise 3. *Translate these educational terms :*

direct method _____ individual method _____

discovery method _____ integrative method _____

discussion method _____ laboratory method _____

experimental method _____ lecture method _____

global method _____ logical method _____

UNIT 41

THE AIMS OF EDUCATION

CULTURE is activity of thought, and receptiveness to beauty and humane feeling. Scraps of informa-tion have nothing to do with it. A merely well-informed man is the most useless bore on God's earth. What we should aim at producing is men who possess culture and expert knowledge in some special direction. Their expert knowledge will give them the ground to start from, and their cul-ture will lead them as deep as philosophy and as high as art. We have to remember that the val-uable intellectual development is self-development and that it mostly takes place between the ages of sixteen and thirty. As to training, the most impor-tant part is given by mothers before the age of twelve. A saying due to Archbishop Temple illus-trates my meaning. Surprise was expressed at the success in after-life of a man, who as a boy at Rugby had been somewhat undistinguished. He answered, " it is not what they are eighteen, it is what they become afterwards that matters."

In training a child to activity of thought, above all things we must beware of what I will call "inert ideas" — that is to say, ideas that are merely received into the mind without being utilised, or tested, or thrown into fresh combinations.

In the history of education, the most striking phe-nomenon is that schools of learning, which at one epoch are alive with a ferment of genius, in a succeding generation exhibit merely pedantry and rou-tine. The reason is, that they are overladen with inert ideas. Education with inert ideas is not only useless: it is, above all things, harmful — *Corruptio optimi, pessima..* Except at rare intervals of intel-lectual ferment, education the past has been rad-ically infected with inert ideas. That is the reason why uneducated clever women, who have seem much of the world, are in middle life so much the most cultured part of the community. They have been saved from this horrible burden of inert ideas. Every intellectual revolution which has ever stirred humanity into greatness has been a passionate pro-test against insert ideas. Then, alas, with pathetic ignorance of human psychology, it has proceeded by some educational scheme to bind humanity afresh with inert ideas of its own fashioning.

Let us now ask how in our system of education we are to guard against this mental dryrot. We enunciate two educational commandments, "Do not teach too many subjects, "and again, "what you each, teach thoroughly."

The result of teaching small parts of a large number of subjects is the passive reception of dis-connected ideas, not illumined with any spark of vitality. Let the main ideas which are introduced into a child's education be few and important, and let them be thrown into every combination possible. The child should make them his own, and should understand their application here and now in the circumstances of his actual life. Form the very beginning of his education, the child should experi-ence the joy of discovery. The discovery which he has to make, is that general ideas give an under-standing of that stream of events which pours through his life, which is his life.

Helpful Vocabulary :

well-informed man	رجل مُطَّلِع
useless bore	مُضجِرٌ عديم الفائدة
expert knowledge	معرفة متخصصة
intellectual development	نمو فكري
to take place	يحدث
as to training	بالنسبة للتدريب
a saying due to	قول يُنْسَبُ إلى
somewhat undistinguished	مغمور نوعاً ما
history of education	تاريخ التربية
the most striking phenomenon	الظاهرة الأبرز
above all things	الأهم من كل الأمور
except at rare intervals	باستثناء فترات نادرة
radically infected with	جَذرياً مصابٌ بـ
in middle life	في وَسَط العمر
horrible burden	عبء ثقيل
intellectual revolution	ثورة فكرية
passionate protest	احتجاج غاضب
bind humanity afresh	يُكَبِّل البشرية من جديد
to guard against	يحترز من
educational commandments	وصايا تربوية
teach thoroughly	عَلَّم بإتقان

Exercise 1 . *Translate the previous passage into Arabic.*

Exercise 2. *Fill in this table with the suitable English derivatives whenever possible, and write down the Arabic equivalents of all the words.*

Verb		Noun		Adjective	
English	**Arabic**	**English**	**Arabic**	**English**	**Arabic**
inform					
		beauty			
bore					
possess					
		expert			
				active	
start					
surprise					
		mother			
				fresh	
infect					
		reason			
				cultured	
proceed					
		education			
				horrible	
		psychology			
				passionate	

Exercise 3. *Translate these educational terms :*

look and say method	_____	problem method	_____
narration method	_____	problem-solving method	_____
objective method	_____	project method	_____
observation method	_____	quantitative method	_____
phonic method	_____	scientific method	_____

179

UNIT 42

TRAINING

Large number of people still basic education and training opportunities. But the proportion of the developing world is overwhelming educational systems. The demand for education far outstrips resources. The financial squeeze between even more restricted budgets and ever larger pupil cohorts further drains programmes of whatever quality they possess because instructional essentials cannot be provided. Policy makers are faced with the hard choice of opting for quality rather than expansion. Because both cannot be provided. In some cases the improvement of training quality will mean consolidating institutions and phasing out marginal programmes in order to generate funds. Despite increasing demand for training, there really is no choice: quality improvement has to take precedence over programme expansion. As Behrman and Birdsall (1983) caution:

> … due to the failure to control for quality, advocacy of expansion without explicit concern for quality improvement is misguided— and the actual return from expanding quantity of schooling at current quality levels will be much less than anticipated .

In low-quality programmes, student achievement levels are often so low that the investment yields little return (Fuller, 1985). Student cannot get and hold jobs because they have little to offer employers— their skills are no different from what can be learned informally on the street or in the workplace. To justify expenditures, student achievement levels must be sufficiently high to offset programme cost, otherwise the investment is poor one .

Low-quality programmes, in the long run, actually cost more than high-quality programmes. Due to hard use and inadequate maintenance and repair, the capital equipment deteriorates rapidly, and has to be replaced before it can be sufficiently amortized to yield reasonably low unit training costs

(Herschbach, 1985). For this reason, the cost of training may be prohibitively high, considerably exceeding costs that would be tolerated even in more affluent countries. Some of the poorest countries may have the highest training costs because of an inability to maintain tools, machinery and equipment adequately to achieve sufficiently high and long use.

Quality improvement depends in part on formulating effective policies; it also depends upon developing adequate administrative and management capabilities. But, most of all, it depends upon classroom inputs which impact strongly on student achievement. By strengthening these inputs, cost savings can be realized because the level of investment in elements unrelated to student achievement can be reduced (Fuller, 1985) .

Another increasingly important issue is the change in skill requirements due largely to worldwide competition (Watanabe, 1986). Higher level skill requirements imply higher quality training.

While technological change is certainly altering production techniques at an unprecedented rate, as Dougherty (1989) suggests, the more potent force of change is the advent of an international market system which opens local production to worldwide competition . There is intense international pressure to increase productivity and improve quality while decreasing cost in those parts of the economy exposed to international competition. Workers design, use and maintain more sophisticated production technology.

The full effects of technological change and international competition on training and work are unknown. One result is greater demand for highly skilled workers competent in organizational, control, maintenance, programming and technical service skills. There is greater need for cognitive skills, and less for manual, production and trade skills (Afthan, 1985). But even in cases where "traditional skills" are used with less sophisticated production technology, there is greater emphasis on improving productivity and quality. The relevant trade-off is "... between the quality of training provision, and the numbers trained with quality requiring greater priority than has been accorded in the past." (Dougherty. 1989. P. 22) .

The "success" of a particular training alternative is conditioned by the country context in which it is placed (Herschbach, 1985). While relative cost is important for investment decisions, it may not be the only __or most useful__variable to consider when making decisions.

Helpful Vocabulary :

basic education	التربية الأساسية
training opportunities	فرص التدريب
proportion of youth	نسبة الشباب
developing world	العالم النامي
instructional essentials	أساسيات التدريس
policy makers	صانعو السياسات ، راسمو السياسات
the hard choice	الاختيار الصعب
training quality	نوعية التدريب
to generate funds	لتوفير الأموال
take precedence over	تنال الأفضلية على
to justify expenditures	لتبرير النفقات
in the long run	في المدى البعيد
inadequate maintenance	صيانة غير كافية
considerably exceeding costs	يفوق التكاليف بكثير
quality improvement	تحسين النوعية
formulating effective policies	صياغة سياسات فاعلة
classroom inputs	مُدْخَلات صَفِّيَّة
cost savings	توفيرات في التكاليف
worldwide competition	منافسة عالمية
production techniques	أساليب الإنتاج
unprecedented rate	معدّل غير مسبوق
skilled workers	عُمَّال مَهَرَة

Exercise 1 . *Translate the previous passage into Arabic.*

Exercise 2. *Fill in this table with the suitable English derivatives whenever possible, and write down the Arabic equivalents of all the words.*

Verb		Noun		Adjective	
English	**Arabic**	**English**	**Arabic**	**English**	**Arabic**
		population			
restrict					
		proportion			
		expansion			
demand					
compete					
		programme			
				explicit	
		release			
provide					
		repair			
				anticipated	
control					
		decrease			
				adequate	
replace					
		increase			
deteriorate					

Exercise 3. *Translate these educational terms :*

sentence method   _____   study method   _____

sight method   _____   survey method   _____

instructional method   _____   statistical method   _____

Socratic method   _____   teaching method   _____

research method   _____   subjective method   _____

UNIT 43

THE ART OF TEACHING

IT IS difficult to write a book on the art of teaching, because the subject is constantly changing. There are dif-ferent way of teaching in different countries of the world, at any one time. Methods in any one country alter every generation or so, as the structure and ideals of society alter. One man will think of as a priv-ilege, work hard and save money to go to the university, and treasure all the knowledge he can get. Thirty years later his son may despise education, resist schooling, waste his time at college, and teach his children to hate books. Thirty years more, and the children will be eagerly educating themselves, perhaps in an unorthodox or wrongheaded way, perhaps late in life or without entering any educational institution, but still with a gen-uine hunger for learning. Each of these generations needs a different kind of teaching.

Then again, there are thousands of different things to learn and learn and teach: so many that you might well ask whether they could all be brought under one system. Is there anything in common between a mother teaching a baby how to talk, a schoolmaster teaching a boy history, a trainer teaching a boxer how to feint, and a foreman teaching a crew of laborers how to lay a road? Even in one country, schools and universities teach a bewildering variety of thing. From simple addition to higher physics from dancing to brain-surgery. And over the whole world, with its thousands of schools and hundreds of uni-versities, how many different subjects are being taught? Today, for instance, a boy is learning the Koran by heart. Another is working at calculus, and a third at double-

Stopping on the violin. Another is practicing pole-vault-ing, and another is reading a manual on demolition work in underground warfare. A girl in Ecuador is being taught lacemaking by Sister Teresa, a girl in India is memorizing the teachings of Gandhi, and a girl in Japan is learning the symbolic meanings of flower-arrangements.

All these subjects, and thousands more, are taught in schools. But a great deal of teaching is done outside school. Some things—and some of the most important things—are taught by mothers and fathers to their chil-dren. This kind of teaching begins as soon as the bay teaches for a knife and his mother takes it away. Not, it begins earlier than that. It really beings when the baby gives his first cry and is first answered. In those days, before he can even hear or see properly, hi is finding our something about the world and himself, he is communi-cating and being answered, he is exerting his will and being victorious or controlled or frustrated, he is being taught to suffer, to fear, to love, to be happy, or to be violent. His mind is being made. Such teaching goes on at a very obscure level, deep down among the founda-tions. We have all experienced it, and forgotten it. But it is none the less crucially important because it is buried so deep. You know how easy it is for a baby to slice his hand open with a knife or scald his leg with a kettle. The scar is still there, forty years later. Many of the twisted minds and crippled characters in the world were made by careless parents who kept their children away from knives and fires, but put permanent scars on their souls.

All through school, and for years after school, parents continue to teach their children. They do so whether they want to or not. The father who never says more than "Hello" to his son and goes out to the nearest bar every evening is teaching the boy just as emphatically as though he were standing over him with a strap. It is a very tricky business, teaching. He may not be teaching his son to drink and neglect responsibilities. The boy may turn out to be a thin ascetic devoted to long plans and hard work, like Shaw and Joyce. But, for good or ill, the father is teaching him *something*. Many fathers either don't know this, or don't care. Yet it is impossible to have children without teaching them.

Helpful Vocabulary :

art of teaching	فن التعليم
constantly changing	متغير باستمرار
alter every generation	تتبدَّل كُلَّ جيلٍ
resist schooling	يقاوم التعليم
educational institution	مؤسسة تربوية
genuine hunger for learning	شَغَفٌ حقيقي بالتعلُّم
crew of laborers	مجموعة من العمال
anything in common	أي شيء مشترك
brain surgery	جراحة الدماغ
learn by heart	يتعلَّم عن ظَهْر قلب ، يحفظُ غَيْباً
underground warfare	الحرب تحت الأرض
teachings of Ghandi	تعاليم غاندي
flower arrangements	تنسيقات الأزهار
as soon as	حالما
first cry	الصيحة الأولى ، الصرخة الأولى
none the less	بالرغم من ذلك
twisted minds	عقول ملتوية
crippled characters	شخصيات مريضة
careless parents	والدون غير مبالين
as emphatically as though	بنفس القوة كأنه
find out	يكتشف
obscure level	مستوى غامض

Exercise 1 . *Translate the previous passage into Arabic.*

Exercise 2. *Fill in this table with the suitable English derivatives whenever possible, and write down the Arabic equivalents of all the words.*

Verb		Noun		Adjective	
English	**Arabic**	**English**	**Arabic**	**English**	**Arabic**
		hunger			
		mother			
				crucial	
		flower			
				obscure	
bury					
		parent			
				victorious	
				cripple	
devote					
hate					
		practice			
				constants	
		treasure			
				emphatic	
force					
		labor			
				educational	

Exercise 3. *Translate these educational terms :*

test-retest method   ——————   word method   ——————

telling method   ——————   microteaching   ——————

unit method   ——————   middle childhood   ——————

whole method   ——————   middle adulthood   ——————

UNIT 44

ERRORS AS POSITIVE
AID TO LEARNING

Some good pedagogical reasons have been suggested for regarding errors made by learners of a foreign language leniently but the most important reason is that the error itself may actually be a *necessary* part of learning a language .

FIRST LANGUAGE ACQUISTION

There has been a great deal of research in the field of first language acquisition. (A good introduction to the study of how people learn to use their mother tongue is de Villiers and de Villiers 1979.) One thing which now seems quite clear is that at some stages of learning their mother tongue, children make guesses about the forms of their language and these guesses are based on the information that they already have about the language. For example, most children growing up and learning English as their mother tongue produce the form 'goed' at some stage for 'went'. Now this, viewed from the perspective of adult grammar, can be called a mistake: it is not the form that an adult or older child would use. However, it can also be regarded as an informed guess, based on the observation that in English the simple past tense is formed in the majority of cases with -ed. (The child could not describe what he was doing in these terms of course, but observation of his language behaviour would lead to this conclusion.)

DIFFERENT TYPES OF 'ERROR'

It would be useful at this stage to distinguish between different types of anomalous language behaviour: the error, the mistake and the lapse. Let us calla systematic deviation, when a learner has not learnt something and consistently 'gets it wrong', an **error**. As mentioned above, a child acquiring his own language sometimes consistently makes the same error. In the same way, when a learner of English as a second or foreign language makes an error systematically, it is because he has not learnt the correct form. A common example is using the infinitive with 'to' after the verb 'must' (eg 'I must to go to the shops'). Let us suppose that the learner knows the verbs want (+ to), need (+ to) and perhaps ought (+ to); by analogy the then produces must (+ to). Until he has been told otherwise, or until be notices that native speakers do not produce this form, he will say or write this quit consistently.

Once a learner has noticed or been taught that in English the verb 'must' does not follow the same pattern as some of the other modal 'verbs, there may well be a period during which he produces 'he must go' and ' he must to go'. Sometimes he will use one form and sometimes the other, quite inconsistently. This inconsistent devia- tion we shall call a mistake: sometimes the learner 'gets it right' but sometimes he makes a mistake and uses the wrong form.

There is another type of wrong usage which is neither a mistake nor an error and can happen to anyone at any time. This is a **lapse**, which may be due to lack of concentration, shortness of memory, fatigue, etc. A lapse bears little relation to whether or not a given form in the language has been learnt, has not been learnt or is in the process of being learnt. Native speakers suffer lapses in the same way as lear-ners of the language; a recent example was a presenter of BBC's Radio 4 who said 'chieving to astrive' instead of 'striving to achieve'.

Many teachers may feel that there is another type of common 'mistake': a **careless slip**, caused by the learner's inattentiveness in class. In fact, by referring to any king of unacceptable or inappropri-ate from as 'carless' we are pre-judging the cause and blaming the learner for it. To be realistic, we must admit that classrooms are not always populated by the idea, motivated, attentive students we would hope for. But can we call a learner careless who produces the following utterance: ' That is the man that I saw him last Friday' after he has worked at sentences demonstrating relative clauses?

Helpful Vocabulary :

pedagogical reasons	أسباب تعليمية
first language acquisition	اكتساب اللغة الأولى
mother tongue	اللغة الأم
make guesses about	يُحدثون تخميناتٍ بشأن
produce X for Y	ينتجون س عِوَضاً عن ص
adult grammar	قواعد البالغين
informed guess	تخمين ذكيّ
based on the observation that	قائمٌ على ملاحظةٍ أنَّ
in the majority of cases	في أغلب الحالات
as mentioned above	كما ذُكِرَ أعلاه
by analogy	بالقياس
be told otherwise	يُخْبِرُ خلاف ذلك
inconsistent deviation	انحراف غير متَّسق
in the same way as	بالطريقة نفسها مِثل
learner's inattentiveness	عدم انتباه المتعلّم
recent example	مثال غريب
pre-judge the cause	نُقَرِّرُ السبب مُسبقاً
to be realistic	لنكون واقعيين
relative clauses	جُمَيَلات الصِّلة
possible explanations	تفسيرات ممكنة
due to	نظراً لِ ، بسبب

Exercise 1 . *Translate the previous passage into Arabic.*

Exercise 2. *What is the opposite of each word, showing Arabic equivalent ? The initial letter of the opposite is given. .*

foreign		n		
reason		r		
first		I		
present		p		
learner		t		
consistent		i		
attentive		i		
deny		a		
older		y		
behavior		m		
majority		m		

UNIT 45

SOCIAL MOVEMENTS

SOCIOLOGISTS are often accused of using unnecessary jargon. Certainly, some of them are prone to 'sociologese', the preference for abstruse and abstract terms rather than for simple commonsense words. All at times, employ tecnnical phrases, the meaning of which cannot be comprehended immediately by the general reader. Yet, for the most part, the vocabulary of sociology is still taken directly from everyday usage, in spite of the dis-advantages which this practice entails; for it is not always realised that the simple language of the vernacular often results in serious misunderstandings, mot only between people generally but also between sociologists themselves. The term 'social movement', or more elliptically 'movement' with an ostensibly clarifying ad-jective, is a splendid case in point. So loose and slipshod has the employment of these words become that they seem capable nowa-days of application any kind of group activity whatsoever. The *Oxford English Dictionary*, indeed, defines a movement as 'a course or series of actions and endeavours on the part of a body of persons, moving or tending more or less continuously toward some special end', which, for the sociologist, does not distinguish a social behaviour, con-sidered over a period of time. The point is that the regular habit of taking as of equal sociological merit every phenomenon, which somebody or other has named a social movement, results in general debasement of the concept for fruitful sociological pur-poses. Some conceptual refinement is an urgent necessity, there-fore, if sociologists are going to make any contribution to under-standing what is peculiar to those forms of group behaviour which differentiates them in a special 'movement' sense from ail other forms.

Form time to time, of course, this problem has been duly realised. Heberle, for example, has emphasised that.

> social movements are a specific kind of concerted-action groups; they last longer and are more integrated than mobs, masses and crowds, and yet are not organised like political

clubs and other associations … Group consciousness, that is, a sense of belonging and of solidarity among member of a group, is essential for a social movement, although empirically it occurs in various degrees … By this criterion social movements are distinguished from' social trends' which are often referred to as movements and are the result of similar but uncoordinated action of many individuals (]18 [p.439). [2]

Similarly, Blumer has distinguished between 'spatial movements', such as mass migration, and 'collective enterprises to establish a new order of life' (]4 [p. 199), whereas Turner and Killian prefer the tern 'quasi-movements' to cover migrations and similar phenomena on the ground that they 'possess some but not all of the characteristics of a movement' (]33 [pp.308-9) At this level the discussion is almost purely verbal and degenerates into 'definitions' mere typologies, taxonomies and natural histories. The alternative, clearly, is to locate the phenomena in question in a theoretical framework of general sociological significance.

The fact that this has not yet been achieved is probably why sociologists continue to fall into the trap of attempting to write about social movements in the same vague ways that they are referred to by the public generally, and why the sociology of social movements is so unsatisfactory. As Killian put it in 1964, 'social movements are conventionally regarded as part of the subject-matter of collective behaviour, but they might just as well be viewed as an aspect of social change. The field of collective be-haviour, however, has been a neglected area of sociology, and in the study of social change, social movements have received relatively little emphasis' (]22[p.426). Why should this be ? The twentieth century-a century which has experienced two world wars, frequent violent revolutions, and a continuous clash be-tween the advocates of numerous social doctrines, of which socialism, communism, fascism and nationalism are only the most manifest- is above all the century of social movements, as well as the century of sociology. Why, then, have sociologists not found a more important place for them in their analyses of social pro-cesses ? In essence, Killian's further point, that this is because men and groups have so often been regarded by sociologists as the creatures rather than the creators of social change', touches on the crucial issue, but it needs further elaboration.

In an earlier attack on the problem with Ralph Turner]33 [Killian defined 'collective behaviour' as 'the behaviour of collectivities', that is, groups 'characterised by the spontaneous development of norms and organization which contradict or re-interpret the norms and organisation of the society'.

Helpful Vocabulary :

at times	أحياناً
technical phrases	عبارات تِقْنيّة
general reader	القارئ العادي
for the most part	في الجانب الأغلب
everyday usage	الاستعمال اليومي
social movement	حركة اجتماعية
group activity	نشاط جماعي
social behavior	سلوك اجتماعي
over a period of time	على مدى فترات من الوقت
conceptual refinement	تنقية المفاهيم
urgent necessity	ضَرورة مُلِحَّة
any contribution to	أية مساهمة في
from time to time	من حينٍ لآخَر
group consciousness	الوعي الجماعي ، الإحساس الجماعي
sense of belonging	الشعور بالانتماء
sense of solidarity	الشعور بالتضامن
by this criterion	بهذا المعيار
mass migrations	هجرات جماعية
quasi-movements	أشباه حركات
on the ground that	على أساس أنَّ
phenomena in question	الظواهر موضع البحث
conventionally regarded	يُنْظَرُ إليها تقليدياً

194

Exercise 1 . *Translate the previous passage into Arabic.*

Exercise 2. *Fill in this table with the suitable English derivatives whenever possible, and write down the Arabic equivalents of all the words.*

Verb		Noun		Adjective	
English	**Arabic**	**English**	**Arabic**	**English**	**Arabic**
accuse					
				simple	
		concept			
				necessary	
define					
				abstract	
cover					
		period			
				immediate	
establish					
		name			
				equal	
locate					
		contribution			
				peculiar	
collect					
		migration			
				verbal	
		emphasis			
individualize					
		discussion			

Text Sources

Unit 1. Stevick, E. W. *Teaching and Learning Languages* . Cambridge : Cambridge University press, 1993 . (pp.21 - 22) .

Unit 2. Priestly, J. B. *Literature and Western Man* . London : Mercury Books, 1992 . (pp. 20 - 21) .

Unit 3. Roberts, E. V. *Writing about Literature* . New York : Prentice Hall, 1994 . (pp. 2 - 3) .

Unit 4. Saunders, J. J. *A History of Medieval Islam* . *London* Routledge and Kegan Paul , 1995 . (pp. 1 - 2) .

Unit 5. Dowse, R. E. *Political Sociology* . New York : John Wiley & Sons , 1992 . (pp. 16 - 17) .

Unit 6. Rixon, S. *How to Use Games in Language Teaching* . London : Macmillan, 1992 . (pp. 1 - 3) .

Unit 7. Groves, N. J. *Geography Teaching* . London : Longman, 1992 . (pp. 2 - 3) .

Unit 8. Finch, R. J. *Practical Geography* . London : Evans Brothers Ltd, 1995 . (pp. 15 - 17) .

Unit 9. Wu-chi, L. *A Short History of Confucian philosophy.* New York : Dell Publishing Co, 1994 . (pp. 36 - 37) .

Unit 10. Welty, P. T. *The Asians.* New York : J. B. Lippincott Co, 1993 . (pp. 6 - 7) .

Unit 11. McRae, J. *Literature with a small ' I '* . London : Macmillan Publishers, 1991 . (pp. 120 – 121) .

Unit 12. Jacobsen, J. A. *Political science*. New York : Barnes & Noble, Ind., 1995 . (p. 15 - 16) .

Unit 13. Deiro, J. A. *Teaching with Heart* . California : Corwin press, Inc., 1996 . (pp. 2 - 3) .

Unit 14. Zverev, I. D. *Teaching Methods in the Soviet School* . Paris: UNESCO, 1993 . (pp. 22 – 23).

Unit 15. Birch, A. & Malim, T. *Developmental Psychology* . Bristol: Intertext Ltd., 1998 . (pp. 161 - 162) .

Unit 16. Spiro, H. J. *World Politics* . Illinois : The Dorsey Press, 1996 . (pp. 161 – 162) .

Unit 17. Bugelski, B. R. *psychology of Learning* . New York : Henry Holt and Co, 1996 . (pp. 1 - 2) .

Unit 18. Sinclair , H. C. *Psychology for Nurses* . London : The English Language Book Society, 1992 . (pp. 1 - 2) .

Unit 19. Incorporated Association of Assistant Masters in Secondary Schools . *Memorandum on the Teaching of Geography* . London : George Philip & Sons. Ltd ., 1996 .

Unit 20. Minshull, R. *An Introduction to Models in Geography* . London : Longman, 1990 . (pp. 1 - 2) .

Unit 21. Bailey, F. G. *politics and Social Change* . California : University of California Press, 1997 . (pp. 107 - 108) .

Unit 22. Cole, M. *A Guide to Modern politics* . London : Victor Gollancz Ltd, 1994 . (pp. 13 - 14) .

Unit 23. Grazia, A. *politics and Government* . New York : Collier Books, 1999 . (pp. 55 - 57) .

Unit 24. Abercrombie, L. *principles of Literary Criticism* . London : High Hill Books, 1990 . (pp. 21 - 22) .

Unit 25. Copleston. F. *A History of philosophy* . New York : Image Book, Inc., 1998 . (pp. 9 - 10) .

Unit 26. Windelbanel, W. *History of Ancient philosophy* . Dover : Dover Publication, Inc., 1996 . (pp. 1 - 2) .

Unit 27. Miller, D. C. *Industrial Sociology* . New York : Harper & Row, Publisher, 1995 . (pp. 3 - 4) .

Unit 28. Eggleston, J. *Contemporary Research in the sociology of Education* . London : Methuen & Co Ltd., 1994 . (pp. 1 - 2) .

Unit 29. Mess, H. A. *Social Structure* . London : George Allen & Unwin Ltd, 1993 . (7 – 8) .

Unit 30. Terrasse. H. *History of Morocco* . Casablanca : Editions Atlantides, 1992 . (pp. 2 - 3) .

Unit 31. Sartre. J.P. *What is literature* ? London : Methuen & Co Ltd, 1991 . (pp. 26 - 27) .

Unit 32. McDouyall, B. S. *Literature and the Art* . Chins : Foreign Languages Press, 1993 . (pp. 1 - 2) .

Unit 33. Abbate, F. *American Art*. London : Octopus Books, 1992 . (pp. 7 - 8) .

Unit 34. Pennington, M. C. *phonology in English Language Teaching*. London : Longman, 1996 . (pp. 22 - 23) .

Unit 35. Burchfield, R. *The English Language* . Oxford : Oxford University Press, 1995 . (pp. 137 - 138) .

Unit 36. Eysenck, H. J. Sense and Nonsense in Psychology. London : Penguin
          Books, 1995 . (pp. 303 - 309) .

Unit 37. Maltz, M.   *Psycho-Cybrnetics* . New York : Prentice-Hall, inc, 1990
          . (pp. 2 - 3) .

Unit 38. Kline, P. *psychology Exposed.* London : Routledge, 1998 . (pp. 13 -
          14) .

Unit 39. Dixon, J. *Growth through English* . Oxford : Oxford
          University Press, 1995 . (pp. 9 - 11) .

Unit 40. Battle, J. A.   *The New Idea in Education* . New York :
          Harper & Row, Publishers, 1998 . (pp. 20 - 21) .

Unit 41. Whitehead, A. N. *The Aims of Education.* London : Ernest Benn
          Ltd, 1990 . (pp. 1 - 2) .

Unit 42. Education Development Center . *Education and Training in the
          1990s* . New York : United Nations Publications, 1990 . (pp. 35 - 36)
          .

Unit 43. Highet, G. *The Art of Teaching* . New York : Vintage Books,
          1990 . (pp. 3 - 4) .

Unit 44. Norrish, J . *Language Learners and Their Error* . London :
          Macmillan press, 1993 . (pp. 6 - 8) .

Unit 45. Banks, J. A. *The Sociology of Social Movements* . London :
          Macmillan, 1992 . (pp. 7 - 3) .

كتب للمؤلف

1. *The Light of Islam*

2. *The Need for Islam*

3. *Traditions of Prophet Muhammad / B1*

4. *Traditions of Prophet Muhammad / B2*

5. *The Truth about Jesus Christ*

6. *Islam and Christianity*

7. *A Dictionary of Islamic Terms : English-Arabic & Arabic-English*

8. *A Dictionary of the Holy Quran : Arabic-English*

9. *Questions and Answers about Islam*

10. *Learn Arabic by yourself*

11. *Simplified English Grammar*

12. *A Dictionary of Education : English-Arabic*

13. *A Dictionary of Theoretical Linguistics : English-Arabic*

14. *A Dictionary of Applied Linguistics : English-Arabic*

15. *Teaching English to Arab Students*

16. *A Workbook for English Teaching Practice*

17. *Programmed TEFL Methodology*

18. *The Teacher of English*

19. *Improve Your English*

20. *A Workbook for English II*

21. *Advance Your English*

22. *The Blessing for Islam*

23. *An Introduction to Linguistics*

24. *Comparative Linguistics : English and Arabic*

25. *A Contrastive Transformational Grammar : English-Arabic*

26. *Why have they chosen Islam ?*